# Favre

• 1996 | Lambeau Field has seen its share of heroes, but none provided as many thrills or inspired as much passion as a freewheeling quarterback from Mississippi.

JOHN BIEVER

• 2006 | The Packers greeted their captain before the season-opener against Chicago.

JOHN BIEVER

4

• 2006 | Seattle's Qwest Field had the look of Lambeau for a late November visit by the Pack.

JONATHAN FERREY/GETTY IMAGES

HE IS NATURAL, AS UNCOMPLICATED AS A SUNDAY AFTERNOON. THE WHEELS AND GEARS OF THE GREAT AMERICAN CELEBRITY MACHINE HAVE YET TO TURN HIM INTO A 6′3″, 220-POUND PLASTIC PACKAGE. EVERYTHING IS STILL NEW.

LEIGH MONTVILLE — *Sports Illustrated, August 23, 1993*

COURTESY OF THE FAVRE FAMILY

BIKE

FAVRE GROWS ANIMATED, LEANING FORWARD. "I DON'T KNOW HOW IT'S GOING TO END, BUT I DO KNOW THIS: THROWING A TOUCHDOWN PASS FOR THE GREEN BAY PACKERS IS PRETTY NEAT. EVERY ONE OF THEM WAS A HELLUVA LOT OF FUN."

ALAN SHIPNUCK — *Sports Illustrated, December 10, 2007*

WALTER IOOSS JR.

1957-2007
NFL

ISBN 10: 1-60320-022-3 • ISBN 13: 978-1-60320-022-6 • LIBRARY OF CONGRESS CONTROL NUMBER: 2008901214 • SPORTS ILLUSTRATED BOOKS IS A TRADEMARK OF TIME INC.

JOHN BIEVER

*Editor*
MARK MRAVIC

*Designer*
STEVEN HOFFMAN

*Photo Editor*
CRISTINA SCALET

*Copy Editor*
KEVIN KERR

*Associate Designer*
JOSH DENKIN

*Reporter*
ADAM DUERSON

*Assistant Photo Editor*
JENNIFER GRAD

# INTRODUCTION

## BY PETER KING

HAVE COVERED Brett Favre throughout his pro career, and when people ask, "What's Favre really like?" I might tell a story about his dead-on imitation of Billy Bob Thornton's character in *Sling Blade,* or about the time on a hunting trip when I heard him cooing, "Here grousie-grousie-grousie." Or I might tell this story. ✦ Ten years ago Green Bay was preparing to play Denver in Super Bowl XXXII in San Diego, and the seven previous times that I had covered the Packers, I had either dined or visited with Favre the Friday before each game—and Green Bay had won every time. On the Monday before the big game, I reminded him of this. "Well then, we've got to go out Friday night," he said. "Find a good place." Then he thought for a second. "Do me a favor. Can you find a girl you might know, around Brittany's age? She'd hate it, being the only kid

BILL FRAKES (PORTRAITS LEFT AND FOLLOWING PAGES)

ALL 4 ONE Devotees displayed their Favre fervor before a December '98 game at Lambeau.

at a diner with all the adults." Brittany Favre, his daughter, was almost nine.

It just so happened that my best friend from college, Dan Squiller, lived in San Diego and had a nine-year-old daughter, Brooke, and the Super Bowl was the biggest thing ever to hit town in her young life. Would she like to go to dinner with Brett Favre and his family? "Yeaaahhh!!!" she said, and even skipped a friend's birthday party to go. When the Favre party of 20 assembled at a La Jolla restaurant, Brooke and Brittany started chatting like new best friends, and Brett couldn't have been more pleased.

"Hey, Brooke," Brett said, "what'd you do in school today?"

"Studied Spanish, I guess. Lots of Spanish," said Brooke, who attended a bilingual magnet school. "Everybody's talking about the Super Bowl, though."

"What do you want to do with your life?" he said.

"Be a marine biologist, I think."

"You have a boyfriend?" he said.

No reply. Just a lot of blushing.

And so Brooke, who'd arrived very nervous, was part of the extended family now. She and Brittany giggled a lot, talked about how they'd redecorate their rooms if their lame parents would only let them. They got a kick out of Brett's ordering the sliced ostrich, along with tenderloin of Texas antelope. "I can just hear the announcers on Sunday," Brett said. *"Favre's a little under the weather today. Must be antelope poisoning."*

As we got up to leave, Brooke got a mischievous look in her eye and asked me for a penny. "Hey, Brett," she said, "here's your lucky penny for Sunday. You know, 'Find a penny, pick it up, all the day you'll have good luck.' Carry this with you, and you'll win." He thanked her and put the penny in his pocket. Brooke asked for only one thing: to have her picture taken with Brett and me.

Fast-forward 48 hours. Denver 31, Green Bay 24. In the postgame interview

area, Favre spotted me and reached inside his high right sock. He pulled out a very sweaty penny. "Tell Brooke sorry," he said with a wry smile. "I guess it wasn't very lucky for me today."

"You're kidding!" I said. "You had that penny in your sock all game?"

"Of course," he said. "She said it'd be lucky."

DON'T ASK ME HOW I COULD FORGET, BUT I NEVER told Brooke what happened to the penny—until I phoned her just as Favre was about to be named SPORTS ILLUSTRATED's 2007 Sportsman of the Year. ✦ "No way! Oh my God, that's insane!" said Brooke, now a sophomore at Cardiff University in Wales. I asked Brooke (double majoring in Spanish and philosophy) if she remembered much about that night. "Are you kidding? I was *sooooo* stoked! One of my 10 most memorable nights ever! Do you know what I have on my bulletin board here? That photo of me, you and Brett! I look so tiny!"

Then she turned serious. "Before that night, I thought famous people were different. I thought they were a level above us," Brooke said. "But Brett was so normal. How many times can you say you were accepted into a family you'd never met before in a matter of minutes, and such a famous family? It may sound corny, but that night changed the way I look at people forever."

I told Brooke, who doesn't follow the NFL much in Wales, that Favre was receiving SI's highest honor. And I told her I was watching him on TV at that moment, against Dallas, and he was running around just like he did that day 10 years ago in her hometown.

"He is amazing!" she said. And then she paused.

"If he ever retired, how would the NFL replace him?" ✦

—*from* SI, DECEMBER 10, 2007

# BRETT

WALTER IOOSS JR.

Sports Illustrated
FAVRE
The TRIBUTE

MICHAEL
JORDAN
FORTY-FORTY
JOSE CANSECO
LUV MY EAGLES!
Orange Bowl
MIAMI
Jan.1,1988
HNC
HAWKS
HANCOCK NORTH CENTRAL HAWKS
HANCOCK NORTH CENTRAL 9th GRADE FOOTBALL
1984 FOOTBALL SCHEDULE
Tulane

# THE KID FROM KILN

BY LEIGH MONTVILLE

*After exploding onto the NFL scene in his first season with the Packers, Favre was preparing for stardom in his own modest way*

SI, AUGUST 23, 1993

**BRETT FAVRE IS LOOKING FOR A CLEAN GOLF SHIRT.** Two clean golf shirts, actually. He is flying in the morning to Pittsburgh, and that afternoon he is playing golf at Oakmont Country Club, and the day after that he is playing in one of those celebrity benefit things at some other Pittsburgh course. His agent has told him that playing at Oakmont is a big deal. The U.S. Open is played sometimes at Oakmont. To move around a course that famous, a man should be dressed right. The agent is worried that Favre may not be dressed right. The agent knows Favre. ✦ "I think about golf and I think about wearing a T-shirt and cutoffs and sneakers," Favre says. "You know what I mean?" ✦ A golf shirt .... ✦ A golf shirt .... ✦ He is looking through piles of clothes, looking through drawers, looking around and around his room. His room? It is a room from the pages of *Boys' Life*. Sports posters and pennants and memorabilia cover the walls and the ceiling, Charles Barkley dunking next to Joe Montana, who is passing a football, next

JOHN CHIASSON

HOME SCHOOLED Even as a pro, Favre retreated to his boyhood bedroom in the off-season.

to a program from the 1982 Sugar Bowl signed by a collegiate Dan Marino. A picture of Bear Bryant is placed directly above a picture of Jesus Christ. Priorities, perhaps. Bear Bryant is the one wearing the checkered porkpie hat.

"Is this all right?" Favre asks, pulling out a blue golf shirt from one of the piles.

"Is it yours?" his mother, Bonita, asks.

Who's to say for sure? Who knows? The three Favre brothers live in this room—O.K., their room—and the shirt could belong to any one of them. It also could belong to their father, Irvin (the Hammer), or maybe to their sister, Brandi, the reigning Miss Teen Mississippi, or maybe to their aunt, Kay-Kay, or maybe to Bonita or maybe to just about anyone in Hancock County. There's a kid named Clark who has been living in the house for a few weeks now, and Jeff, the youngest brother, back just today from his freshman year at Southern Mississippi, in Hattiesburg, has brought a friend to stay for a few days, and a kid named Mark has been around all day and . . . who knows? Laundry is a problem.

"Brett was wearing my shirt one day," Kay-Kay says. "I told him it was mine. He said it was his. I said, 'Well, that must be true, because you look awfully good in a T-shirt with shoulder pads. . . .' "

"Everybody just wears everybody else's clothes in this house," Bonita says. "It gets confusing. One time I just wrote names on everything, to try to keep down the fights. Well, Brett calls us from Green Bay one day. He got undressed in the locker room. Seems that the word DAD was written across the top of his underpants . . . . "

Blue. Brett decides the shirt must be his. Couldn't be anyone else's. He throws it into his traveling bag. Now he needs to find only one more shirt for the trip. Why is the outside world so complicated? A golf shirt to play golf.

THE HOUSE IS ON IRVIN FARVE ROAD IN KILN, MISS., A DEAD-END dirt road that finishes at a still stretch of water called Rotten Bayou. On a hot day, of which there are many here, a visitor arrives in a small tornado of red dust. Almost 10 years ago the road was named after Brett's dad, which seemed logical since he was the local high school football and baseball coach and no one but Favres and their relatives lived on the road anyway. The sign was misspelled, which is not so bad because that is the way the name is pronounced. People can figure it out.

As for Kiln, the *n* is dropped by local speakers. The town of 7,500 residents usually is called the Kill. The question would be "Where does the hottest young quarterback in the NFL live in the off-season?" The answer would be "The Kill." People can figure it out. This is home.

"People say, 'You're the quarterback of the Green Bay Packers and you still live at home?' " Brett Favre says. "Well, I could be other places, but I can't think of one I'd rather be. Where else could I have so much fun? That's what this is all about. Having fun."

He is 23 years old and as uncomplicated as a Sunday afternoon. Natural. Where else could he fall out of his water bed every day and land in a family party? His grandmother Mee-Maw lives in that little trailer down the road and makes the best gumbo on the Gulf. (Mee-Maw's real name is Izella French, but Brett and his brothers began calling her Mee-Maw and their other grandmother Maw-Maw when they were little. The names stuck.) There always is someone around who will play a little golf or maybe go over to Biloxi or Gulfport and do a little gambling on one of those new paddleboat casinos. There always is someone around to have a beer, to start a barbecue. Where else is every day the Fourth of July?

RONALD C. MODRA

Brett basked in the warmth of Kiln with Brandi, Mee-Maw and Bonita.

"I remember the first long trip I made," Brett says. "Senior year of high school. The class trip. We went from here to New York and Boston. We raised the money ourselves with all kinds of projects. I went to a restaurant, a sandwich place in Boston. The guy said, 'What'll you have?' I told him I guess I'd have a shrimp po'boy. He just looked at me. I tried to explain what a shrimp po'boy was. I wound up with a submarine sandwich."

The wheels and gears of the Great American Celebrity Machine are only now starting to turn. There has not been time yet to turn him into a 6' 3", 220-pound plastic package, to make him accustomed to limousine living and large sums of money and everyday fame. Everything is still new. He basically has had one electric season in the NFL, last year, when he came off the bench for the Packers in their third game and never sat down again, rejuvenating the team, at one time passing for more than 200 yards in each of 11 straight games. The team missed the playoffs only on the final Sunday. He wound up in the Pro Bowl. He showed again and again that he could throw the football. Then he came home.

"Reporters would ask me where I got my arm," he says. "I always thought it was from my father, but now I think I got it from my mother. She got mad at me last summer and threw a pastrami sandwich and hit me in the head. Hard. She really had something on that sandwich."

"I was really mad," says Bonita, who is a special-ed teacher at Hancock County High. "I was running the four swimming pools in the area, in charge of 12 lifeguards. They were driving me crazy, the lifeguards. I told all of them if it started to rain, I would call and tell them whether or not to close the pools for the day. I told them not to call me. I would call them. Well, it started to rain, and this one lifeguard calls me. I was just fuming, and Brett, he's sitting in the kitchen just laughing at me. I had this pastrami sandwich in my hand, and I just let it go, mustard and bread flying all over the place . . . . "

"I didn't even know what pastrami was," Brett says. "Except that it hurt."

The good things that happened in Green Bay and in assorted other stadiums around the country still seem almost touched with magic. The idea that anyone could come from here—this little place six miles from the Gulf of Mexico, where an occasional alligator pokes its head from the bayou—and wind up famous is borderline fantasy. The Packers virtually have handed their team to Favre. They dumped his competition, Don Majkowski, the hottest young quarterback of three years ago, and brought in veteran Ken O'Brien from the New York Jets to add experience and counsel. They went heavy on the free-agent market this off-season, winning the big-money chase for defensive end Reggie White. They are making a run for a division title, making it with a kid quarterback.

This is a different situation for Favre. For the first time in his life he is not an underdog. "I've always had to struggle for what I've got," he says. "I was never recruited for college. No one really wanted me. Coming from down here, nobody knows who you are. Three days before the signing date, I was going to either Pearl River Junior College or Delta State. Southern Miss took me as a defensive back. When I went there as a freshman, I worked out both ways at first. I was the seventh quarterback on the depth chart."

Seventh on the depth chart? He was third by the time his freshman season started. He was playing by the second half of the second game, throwing two touchdown passes to beat Tulane. On his 18th birthday he was starting against No. 1–ranked Florida State, the Florida State fans singing a derisive *Happy Birthday* as his team was pounded by the Seminoles 61–10. He was on his way.

"Southern Miss was a place where everyone had been rejected by the big schools for some reason," he says. "We were the Island of Misfits. We thrived on that. We'd play Alabama, Auburn, and there'd be stories in the papers about how we'd been rejected by them. We'd come out and win the game, and guys would be yelling on the field, 'What's wrong with us now?' It was a great way to play."

As his senior year approached, he was known as a fearless kid who could throw the ball. The Southern Miss offense had been redesigned for his talents. He had completed 79 passes for 1,264 yards and 15 touchdowns. The pro scouts were interested. He was ready for big things. Then he flipped his Nissan Maxima and almost killed himself during the summer before that senior year.

The accident happened in the Kill, less than a mile from his house. Returning from a July afternoon of sun and, sure, fun at Ship Island, he says he was blinded by the lights of another car. He swerved and hit gravel, and when he tried to pull the car back onto the road, it began to flip. His brother Scott was following in another car and later reported that one flip was so high "you could have driven a dump truck underneath the car." Scott broke the front window with a golf club to pull Brett from the wreckage. Brett wound up in the hospital with a concussion, lacerations and a cracked vertebra and, it turned out, complications.

JIMMY CRIBB/WIREIMAGE.COM

Favre's short stint as a Falcon in '91 offered little hint of what was to come.

"I was out of the hospital, and I thought I was O.K.," Brett says. "I wasn't eating much, though, and when I did I was throwing up. I kept having these abdominal pains, and they started to get worse. I went back to the hospital, and they found that a lot of my intestines had died."

Thirty inches of intestine were removed. His recovery had to begin all over again. He reported to Southern Miss in mid-August but still was having trouble eating. Back he went to Kiln, where Mee-Maw's cooking finally got him going. Five weeks after the intestinal surgery he was at Southern Miss again, in uniform, 30 pounds underweight, leading the Golden Eagles to a 27–24 upset over Alabama.

"You can call it a miracle or a legend or whatever you want to," Alabama coach Gene Stallings told reporters afterward. "I just know that on that day, Brett Favre was larger than life."

The Eagles finished the 1990 season at 8–4. Favre, who never was 100% recovered from the surgery, ended up in the Senior Bowl and the East-West Shrine Game. At the Shrine game he more than caught the attention of Ron Wolf, then a scout for the Jets. After the accident a lot of scouts had dropped Favre in their thinking. Wolf still liked the way he threw the ball and also liked the way he took charge, the way he had that gift of making everyone else in a huddle listen and respond. How many leaders does a scout see?

Alas, the Jets already had lost their No. 1 pick by signing Syracuse wide receiver Rob Moore in the supplemental draft. Their first choice in 1991 was in the second round, 34th overall. The Atlanta Falcons picked Favre at number 33 and gave him a three-year contract worth $1.2 million. It wasn't until the next year, when Wolf had moved along to become the Packers' general manager, that he finally could make his move. On Feb. 10, 1992, Wolf traded the Pack's first pick to Atlanta, for which Favre had thrown only five passes all season playing third-string. Wolf was told he was crazy.

" 'Have your lost your mind?' was what most people said," Wolf says. "I just really liked him. He has that unexplainable something about him."

The '92 season turned out better than Favre or even Wolf could have expected. When Majkowski went down with sprained ligaments in his left ankle, the prognosis was that he would miss two weeks, maybe four. Favre came into the lineup, won two games and simply rolled. Natural. He finished with 302 completions for 3,227 yards and 18 touchdowns. He was sixth in the league in completion percentage, third in interception rate.

He also showed durability and resourcefulness. In the first half of his seventh start his left shoulder was separated in a hit delivered by White, then with the Philadelphia Eagles. It was a brutal play. Favre had thrown his pass and could see the collision coming. He turned his body to absorb it. White grabbed his hand and yanked him back the other way to make him vulnerable. The two men landed together. Favre's shoulder was the point of impact. It was a play designed to do what it did—to hurt him, hopefully to put him out of the game—not to stop the pass. He stayed in the game, shot up with a painkiller at halftime, but could not lift his arm as high as his shoulder and could not hand off to the left. The Eagles and the rest of the teams on the Packers' schedule saw his difficulty and worked on it. The shoulder hurt for the rest of the season, but he still played.

"Now Reggie's with us," Favre says. "I talked with him at minicamp. He said he thought for sure he had put me out. I told him I just about thought he had too. Then he put his arm around me. He told me not to worry, that this year we were on the same side. I liked that."

The shoulder, still healing, still hurts. It should be better by the start of the season.

SPORTS ILLUSTRATED," FAVRE SAYS, PACKING FOR THE TRIP TO Pittsburgh. "In my junior year a writer came down to Southern Miss to do an article for SPORTS ILLUSTRATED. He said he wasn't sure the article would be in, but if we beat Florida State in our opener, he was pretty sure it would make it. We go out. We pull the upset. All I'm thinking about the last few minutes on the field is, God, I'm going to be in SPORTS ILLUSTRATED." The article never appeared—Southern Miss went on a four-game losing streak after the upset—but so be it. SPORTS ILLUSTRATED. He will be in there now. It will mention the new house he has added to the colony on Irvin Farve Road. Though there is an apartment on the second floor that he will use sometimes, it is not his house. It is a family house. A party house with a swimming pool. It has changing rooms, a big-screen TV, a pool table and video games, a room with a Jacuzzi, a full kitchen to prepare party foods and a deck large enough to hold as many people as might show up at any one time.

"We've already had parties there," Favre says. "Nothing planned. They just happen. A couple of weeks ago we started on Thursday, and by Saturday there were over 100 people on the deck."

This night's plans seem to be taking shape. Favre is going to New Orleans, where he will take a hotel room so he can make his 6:30 a.m. flight to Pittsburgh. Clark, the friend, is going along for the ride to New Orleans and to spend the night partying. Mark, the other friend, also is going. Jeff, the younger brother, is not going. Back from college, he is going to look around the area for some friends and some action. Scott, the older brother, also is not going, because he is in Hattiesburg taking a real estate course.

Bonita is going down to Mallini's Point Lounge in Pass Christian with Mee-Maw and Mee-Maw's boyfriend. Once he gets cleaned up after a late dinner, Irvin will join them. Mallini's once was owned by Mee-Maw's late husband, Bennie French, who was a local rogue of sorts, a man who managed boxers and had a speakeasy and ran whiskey off the Gulf Coast for Al Capone. Bonita and Irvin once worked at the bar, and Brett and Scott rode their Big Wheels around the pool tables when they were young. Kay-Kay is staying home because she has to go to work early in the morning. Brandi, Miss Teen Mississippi, also is staying home. She is 16 and says she has a lack of dates because Brett and her other brothers say they will seriously injure any date who comes to the door.

Perhaps Brett's own experience has educated him in this regard. He has a four-year-old daughter, Brittany, with Deanna Tynes, whom Brett has been dating since ninth grade. Brittany stays at the house every day while her mother works. Deanna is getting Brittany ready to go home. It is not an awkward situation. In fact, it is quite pleasant. Everyone is making a fuss over Brittany.

"Why would I want to be anywhere else?" Brett says from the middle of the activity. "Why?"

He says he will be home in two days. He has made only two golf commitments for the entire summer, this one and a later tournament in Milwaukee named in honor of Vince Lombardi. The Lombardi tournament makes him nervous. Packers coach Mike Holmgren, who played last year, told him the fairways were lined with spectators. What if they are lined with spectators this year? Favre says he is sure he will hit one of them on the noggin and that the ball will be traveling fast. Favre says that Holmgren was in control of his nerves at the beginning of last year's tournament, but he was paired with Leslie Nielsen, the actor. Nielsen had one of those whoopee cushions, and he made the sound of breaking wind whenever Holmgren was close on the 1st tee. The coach was nervous the rest of the day. "All I hope," Favre says in a down-home Southern accent, "is that I'm not playing with Leslie Nielsen this year."

On to Pittsburgh. The outside world awaits. ✦

# COUNTDOWN

BY PETER KING

*A day-by-day account of Favre's game week provided a revealing look into the head—and the heart—of a quarterback rising to the top of his game*

SI, OCTOBER 30, 1995

**MONDAY: THE AFTERMATH ✦ IT'S JUST AFTER** 8 a.m., and Brett Favre cannot bear the thought of getting out of the four-poster bed he shares with his girlfriend of 10 years, Deanna Tynes. This has nothing to do with the previous night's celebration of his artistic 342-yard passing performance against the Detroit Lions, which consisted of a single light beer. This has everything to do with the throbbing turf toe on his right foot. And the right shoulder he had heard go snap-crackle-pop when it was jammed into the turf 20 hours before. And the lower-back pain he feels every Monday, the lingering result of a lumbar fracture suffered in a 1990 car accident. And the arthritis that he knows is advancing in both hips. And his aching right side, which is the worst of all his ailments. Ten months ago two sections of hard plastic mesh were sewn into the muscle walls in his right side just below his ribs to repair a herniated muscle, a belated casualty of the car crash. His doctors

RICH FRISHMAN

TOP PRIORITY Amid the hubbub of game prep, Brett made time for Brittany, then 6.

said the muscle would take a year to heal completely. Of course Favre couldn't wait that long. And so he must try to ignore the grotesque, egg-shaped growth of plastic and muscle mass that protrudes from his right side. Most of the time he succeeds, except after games, when the side feels as if something is ripping inside him when he moves.

"Deanna," Favre pleads in his Mississippi twang. "Could you please get me an egg sandwich and some hash browns?"

Deanna goes out for some fast-food breakfast. A few minutes later Favre, still in bed, is propped up on his left arm, polishing off his meal. Eating triggers more pain. When he chews, his jaw aches from the brutal helmet-to-helmet hit he took from Pittsburgh Steelers linebacker Greg Lloyd in the preseason.

Finally Favre musters the energy to walk to the bathroom. His left knee is killing him. "God," he says to himself, "I didn't know I hurt that." Then he remembers the kick in the knee that he took against Detroit. He hadn't felt that one until now.

"When he gets up every Monday," Deanna says, "he looks like such an old man." Favre is 26.

At 11 a.m. Favre leaves his house for the two-mile drive to the Packers' training complex at Lambeau Field. There, strength-and-conditioning coach Kent Johnston sets to work on Favre's aching body, guiding him through exercises that include sit-ups and a medicine-ball drill designed to loosen his stiff joints and muscles. "I'm a new man!" Favre announces as he pulls out a plastic bottle from behind Johnston's counter. The label reads MUSASHI. "It's branched-chain amino acids from Australia," Johnston says. "It helps with recovery after a workout." Favre puts two teaspoons of the white powder on his tongue and washes it down with spring water.

Monday is report-card day, and after his session with Johnston, Favre and his two backups, Ty Detmer and T.J. Rubley, join quarterbacks coach Steve Mariucci to review the Lions game.

"We had 12 audibles yesterday—nine good, three not so good," Mariucci says.

"Not bad," says Favre.

"Well," Mariucci says as the videotape shows Favre dropping back to throw, "let's make it 12 good. But there are lots of good things here. Good throws, good rhythm. Now keep both hands together, seven-step, hitch and throw. Good!"

As the day progresses, Mariucci, wide receivers coach Gil Haskell, offensive coordinator Sherm Lewis, offensive line coach Tom Lovat, tight ends coach Andy Reid, offensive assistant Marty Mornhinweg and running backs coach Harry Sydney will formulate the game plan to be used against the Minnesota Vikings. Head coach Mike Holmgren will oversee the blueprint, which will be presented to the Packers' offensive players beginning on Wednesday. On Saturday morning Holmgren and the quarterbacks will meet to review Green Bay's pass plays until they find a collection of plays they like.

RICH FRISHMAN

Favre and Mariucci worked together relentlessly on the practice field and in the film room.

While his assistants focus on the game plan, Holmgren has a disciplinary chore to attend to. He has heard that his two frisky young running backs, second-year man LeShon Johnson and rookie Travis Jervey, are about to get into more trouble. The two share a house out in the Wisconsin sticks, and they have already been cited by the state's Department of Natural Resources for having illegal deer snares in the backyard. That prompted a $200 fine for each player from the DNR. Just last week, while building a fire in his fireplace, Jervey had poured gasoline on the kindling and then struck a match. The fumes and the gas exploded, igniting Jervey. He rolled around on the floor, snuffing out flames that singed his eyebrows and eyelashes and the hair on his arms and legs.

And now, Holmgren has been informed, Jervey and Johnson have ordered a lion from a Texas wildlife distributor. "Just a little one," Johnson says. "And he's had his claws taken out, and his canines. He can't hurt you."

Jervey and Johnson paid $1,000 for the animal, but it hasn't been delivered yet. That's good. "You can't buy a lion," Holmgren says. "No lion." The order is canceled.

Having dismissed the two young players, Holmgren, a patient, genial sort, says, "There's a lot involved in coaching a football team, you know?"

"Maybe we'll get something else," Jervey says after his session with Holmgren. "I think I'd like a tiger."

## TUESDAY: FREE TIME

Tuesday is the players' day off in the NFL, and Favre is going hunting. But first he stops in to see Mariucci, who has been watching tape of the Vikings' 20–17 loss to the Tampa Bay Buccaneers two days earlier. “Look at these new guys,” Mariucci says, indicating cornerback Corey Fuller and safety Orlanda Thomas, two rookies who are starting in the Minnesota secondary. “This is the guy we're going after—the spitter. We like that matchup, Robert Brooks on Fuller.”

Bucs quarterback Trent Dilfer had accused Fuller of spitting in his face during an on-field argument. And now, as tape of the Vikings’ pass coverage in games against the Dallas Cowboys and the Houston Oilers, as well as against Tampa Bay, unfolds on the screen, Favre and Mariucci watch Fuller playing far off the receiver—enough of a cushion, they believe, for Favre to drill completions all day long. Favre begins to think that he will be throwing to the right a lot on Sunday.

Favre came to Green Bay in a 1992 trade with the Atlanta Falcons, and this season is the first in which he has not felt obligated to steer the offense toward one receiver. During the off-season All-Pro wideout Sterling Sharpe retired because of a neck injury. Favre wasn't sad to see him go, even though Sharpe had caught 314 passes over the past three seasons and was on the receiving end of 18 of Favre's 33 touchdown passes in ’94. “I know he was a great player, but we're a better team this year without Sterling,” Favre says. “Last year we'd put so many plays into the game plan designed for Sterling that I'd go back to pass thinking, I've got to get it to Sterling. Now I just go back and read. If the first guy's not free, I go to the next guy. We're spreading the ball among all our receivers.”

At noon Favre leaves the Packers complex for his hunting trip in a caravan that includes his two best friends on the team, tight end Mark Chmura and center Frank Winters, and a local pal, Kevin Burkel. On the road he muses again about Sharpe. “After I signed my big contract [five years, $19 million] last year, we were at practice, and I threw Sterling a deep post. He let it go over his head, but it looked as if he could have had it if he'd really wanted to. He came back to the huddle and said, ‘Hey, if I'm going to run that far down the field, the least you can do is put it on me. Somebody making $19 million ought to be able to throw a good pass.’

“This is in front of everyone. Kind of under his breath, he's saying things like, ‘I can't believe you're making more than me.’ I said, ‘---- you!’ I just went after him. I said, ‘They pay me to throw it. They pay you to catch it. So why don't you just shut up and do what you're told to do.’”

At a private 200-acre hunting and fishing preserve, Favre goes in search of grouse, though not exactly by the book. “Here, grousie! Come on out, grousie!” he calls. The only fauna that respond to Favre's call are a couple of garter snakes.

“Whoa!” he says, jumping back at the sight of the first one. “That s.o.b. was snapping at me. Did you see that? Guys like [Cowboy pass rusher] Leon Lett, I can deal with. Snakes, I can't.”

RICH FRISHMAN

 NO REST Even on an off day, Favre studied film before some R&R with Chmura and Winters.

The group has better luck hooking rainbow trout in the stocked lake. Favre rushes through a fish fry; he has four talk shows to do between 6 and 7 p.m.

## WEDNESDAY: THE PACK'S PLAN

The essence of a game plan is matching what your team does well against what your opponent does badly. With Minnesota up next, Green Bay is in the enviable position of having one of the league's hottest quarterbacks confronting a young secondary that has been allowing opponents to complete 62% of their passes. Late in the day Holmgren tells his staff that he's thinking of being bolder against the Vikes than he has been against them in recent games. Three of the last four Green Bay–Minnesota meetings have been low-scoring, each decided by less than a touchdown. The Packers lost three of them.

Last night Mornhinweg inserted 61 of the Packers' 93 pass plays into each offensive player's playbook. Each play is precisely diagrammed, with notes printed on the side, like "X stays wide!" Holmgren likes to limit the number of pass plays to 100, though he keeps pushing the envelope to see how much Favre can handle. "I want to have 10 new pass plays a week," Holmgren says. "I just think that keeps it interesting for the guys. As long as you're not short-circuiting your quarterback, it keeps things fresh."

One by one, Holmgren's offensive assistants step to the front of a meeting room on the second floor of the Packers complex. Each coach has spent two days watching tape of the Vikings. Now they report on each Minnesota defensive player. Lovat critiques the Vikings linemen, and Sydney dissects the linebackers.

Haskell analyzes the Minnesota secondary. "They've got a second-year guy, a rookie, a rookie and a free agent," he says. "If that was our team, we'd be nervous. If we protect Brett, we'll get some big plays."

Lewis, the offensive coordinator, steps up. "Brett, this is an anxious team," he says of the Vikings. "They like to get a quick start at the snap. Work on your cadence this week. Get them to jump offside, then—boom!—free play. Think home run then. They pride themselves on turnovers. They tackle the football. If we don't turn the ball over, we win the game. Let's have good concentration when we're installing our plays at practice today."

Lovat takes 25 minutes to explain the running plays. Now it's Holmgren's turn. He handles the pass plays every week. He stands at the front of the room, his hands all over a white screen on which an overhead projector is beaming O's and Y's and passing lanes. As Holmgren speaks, the players sit attentively. Winters takes notes on almost every play, and wide receiver Mark Ingram traces a yellow highlighting marker on his routes.

The fourth pass play that Holmgren discusses is called Red Right Slot A Right 322 Scat Y Stick. Red means that the basic Packers personnel group is on the field, with two backs, two wide receivers and a tight end. Right means that tight end Chmura is deployed to that side of the line. Slot means that Brooks lines up four yards outside the left tackle and a step back from the line. A means that halfback Edgar Bennett lines up to the left of the quarterback (B would have him directly behind Favre; C would place him to the right). On this play fullback Dorsey Levens is in the C spot. The second Right means that Bennett will go in motion to that side. The designation 322 means that Favre will take a three-step drop, the left tackle and left guard will go one-on-one with their opponents, and no one will remain in the backfield to pick up a blitzer on the left side or help out if one of the defenders gets free to attack Favre. Scat means the fullback will be a receiver. Y Stick means the tight end runs a simple six-yard down-and-out.

Ingram, lined up wide left, runs a deep decoy route. Levens flares wide out of the backfield to the right. Bennett, after going in motion to the right, sprints upfield at the snap of the ball. Brooks runs an intermediate sideline route. After Favre takes the snap and a three-step drop, he looks first at the fullback running his little flare. If Levens is covered, Favre looks to the tight end. If Chmura is covered, Favre looks to the flanker. "If no one's open," Favre says, "I throw it away or run it. But somebody's almost always open. In 1992 we completed 27 of 32 on this play, and it should have been 29. We had two drops."

Next time you want to scream at your local quarterback, read those last two paragraphs. And then keep in mind that there's a 40-second clock ticking, and that an offensive coordinator is barking into the quarterback's helmet speaker, and that the quarterback has to shout in the huddle to be heard above the crowd. Multiply Red Right Slot A Right 322 Scat Y Stick times 117—that's how many plays Favre and the offense need to memorize for Sunday.

This week Holmgren's favorite play is Red Right Double Stutter Go, which will match Brooks against Fuller, and either Ingram or wideout Anthony Morgan opposite cornerback Dewayne Washington. The receivers will run straight ahead five yards, stop, turn their shoulders as if looking for a pass and then sprint straight downfield, hoping that at least one of the corners will bite on the fake. "Mark home run on this play," Holmgren says to Brooks. "I really like it."

Back home Favre cooks dinner—the spiciest batch of shrimp étouffée and rice north of New Orleans. He then carves a pumpkin with six-year-old daughter, Brittany, before snuggling into bed alongside her and reading a Berenstain Bears story. Then he spends 15 minutes matching plays with Vikings formations.

## THURSDAY: ONE WORD, ATTACK

At 9 a.m. Holmgren strides to the front of the meeting room. "Good morning, men," he says to his 53 players. "I've been doing a lot of thinking about this game. Why is it we always play this team so close and have such trouble scoring? Number 1, they've had a great pass rush. But they didn't score an offensive touchdown against us in two games last year, and we split the two games. We're going to play it differently this week. Offensively, we're going after them."

He turns to Favre. "Brett, the ball's in your hands. I don't want this one to come down to the last two minutes with it 10–10 and a field goal or turnover deciding it. We're going to attack them. Now guys, study the tape. Have a great day of practice. It's going to be a war. Everyone have a good day."

During a quick quarterbacks meeting in Mariucci's office before practice, Mariucci clicks on a tape of Vikings nickel pass coverage. Favre utters some unprintable cracks and mercilessly releases flatulence at Mariucci, Detmer and Rubley, who nonetheless survive to get some work done. At these meetings, 13 of which take place between Monday and Saturday, Favre is the class clown.

Before lunch Favre hits the treadmill and does some aerobics. He takes more Musashi and downs two megavitamins (with a total of 12,000% of the recommended daily allowance of vitamin C), two flaxseed capsules and two fish-oil capsules. "You're nuts, taking all that crap," Winters says as he observes his friend. "The guys who take that stuff are always in the trainers' room. I'm never there. Beer and pizza. That's what you need in this league."

At practice Holmgren sidles up to Favre and says, "I just want you to know: Keith Jackson's probably coming in tonight." Jackson, an All-Pro tight end, had been traded to the Packers by the Miami Dolphins in March but refused to report, citing Green Bay's brutal winters. Now he has relented, and Holmgren wants Favre to help smooth over any anti-Jackson sentiment on the team.

This evening Favre makes a 10 p.m. run to Mariucci's house to give his four-week-old daughter, Brielle, a gift. He takes the sleeping child from her father, cradling her and cooing at her. "Hey, Brielle," he says in his best high-pitched daddy voice. "Horse walks into a bar. Bartender says, 'Hey, why the long face?' "

## FRIDAY: A CHILLY WELCOME

The phone rings at 7:03 a.m. Deanna picks it up, shakes the sleeping Favre and hands him the receiver. "Hi, Brett!" a perky female voice says. "This is WTMJ in Milwaukee calling, and we hear Keith Jackson is signing with the Packers today. We want to know if you have any comment."

No, he says, then turns over to grab another hour of sleep.

Later in the morning, in the locker room, JACKSON 88 appears above an empty locker. Favre seeks out Chmura and points to the tag. Chmura knew this day would come, and he doesn't look upset. Favre drapes his arm around Chmura and says, "Hey, Bud, don't worry. I'm still going to throw you the ball." Favre knows the chemistry in Green Bay is good, and one of his goals today is to make sure no one makes a stink about Jackson.

At practice Jackson drops in line with Chmura and the other tight ends in passing drills. After a session with tight ends coach Reid, Jackson says that the offense is unlike any he has seen. "I feel like I've got to learn Chinese arithmetic," he says, looking pained.

"Men," Holmgren says to his players in a postpractice moment, "I'd like to welcome two new guys—[defensive back] Roderick Mullen, whom we got from the Giants [from their practice squad], and Keith Jackson, whom we got from Little Rock. He's late because we couldn't find him a plane from Little Rock to Green Bay." That's it. The welcome isn't warm. Holmgren wants Jackson to know all isn't forgiven. But Holmgren also wants Jackson to know that he can make it right by producing.

Before the quarterbacks leave for the day, Mariucci hands them their weekly five-page test in which a single element has been omitted from each of 74 different plays. The quarterbacks must fill in the missing information. Then there's a page of "Draw this play" questions, with six drawings required. Favre is correct on 70 of 74 formations—Detmer, the Packers' Einstein, misses three—and draws all his plays right except for a sloppily sketched split-end route.

Before he leaves for the day, Favre hosts a surprise 41st birthday party for Green Bay's mail clerk, Leo Yelle, who is developmentally disabled. The party stuns Yelle, who gets a game jersey from Favre and a duffel bag full of gifts from the team. Favre, the only player at the party, gives Yelle a hug and eats some cake with him. In one corner, two secretaries dab at their eyes.

### SATURDAY: THE SCRIPT

At 9:15 a.m. Holmgren asks for input from the three quarterbacks, Mariucci and Mornhinweg as he draws up his First 15. Bill Walsh began this strategy when he was the coach of the San Francisco 49ers. He scripted the first 15 plays of the game, trying his hardest to stick to it while feeling out the opposition. Since taking over the Packers, Holmgren has taken this a step further, sketching a First 15 for the second half that he fine-tunes during the intermission.

"How do you like Double Stutter Go?" Holmgren asks Favre.

"Love it," Favre says.

"Might be in the First 15. O.K., flea-flicker."

"Let's do it," Mariucci says.

"Second-and-one, first series," Favre says. "C'mon, Mike! Let's go for the jugular."

In closing, Holmgren stares at Favre. This is the last thing he will say to him before Sunday afternoon, because he believes in leaving a quarterback alone before a game. "This game puts pressure on you to make plays. But you've been through that," Holmgren says. "This team believes in what's going on here. This team believes in you. Just be careful with the football and play how you've been playing."

RICH FRISHMAN

Holmgren drew up elaborate game plans but knew his quarterback could freelance at any time.

After one last quarterback meeting, Favre heads home. He has visitors in for the weekend from Louisiana, but they are out when he gets home, shortly before noon. So he sleeps for six hours. Then he reports to the team hotel where all the Packers stay the night before a home game. Holmgren gets to the hotel about 3 p.m., takes a nap and makes his final choices for the First 15.

## SUNDAY: THE PAYOFF

Less than an hour before the game, as Favre throws easily on the field, he is greeted by Tony Dungy, Minnesota's veteran defensive coordinator. "Don't you go putting the ball up too much on us today," Dungy says. "You take it easy on us."

Once the game begins, it is apparent that Dungy's defense is not about to take it easy on Favre. The Vikings blitz from the opening minute. But the quarterback adjusts quickly, and the blitzing hardly alters the carefully crafted Packers' game plan.

Green Bay begins its first series of the game from its 34, and Holmgren runs the first five plays, in order, off the list he devised on Saturday night: Favre to Brooks for nine yards; Bennett off left guard for two; Favre, under a heavy blitz, to Levens on a screen pass for 20; Bennett up the middle for a yard. Then, in the face of a rare cornerback blitz by Washington, Favre sees that safety Charles Mincy is late in moving over to cover Morgan, and Favre throws to him for 22 yards, down to the Minnesota 12.

On the sixth play Favre interrupts the First 15 and audibles from a run to a pass, but he throws incomplete to fourth wideout Charles Jordan. Holmgren now turns to his red-zone list of plays and picks a winner, Fake 95. Favre finds Chmura in a crease between defenders for a touchdown.

On the sideline Favre immediately seeks out Jordan. "If we get that same play again," Favre says, "I'm going to check to the same thing. Only you don't run that slant you just ran. You run the slant-and-go."

Early in the second quarter the Packers have the ball at the Vikings' five. Favre calls the same audible. Jordan runs straight at Fuller, glances back for a Favre pump-fake and then streaks to the right corner of the end zone. Fuller stumbles, and Jordan is all alone when the ball arrives. It is 14–14 at the half.

In the third quarter the Minnesota rush is taking its toll, and Green Bay goes three-and-out on its first two series of the half. With 22 minutes left in the game, Favre is only 12 of 30. But on the next series he is four of five, finishing a 69-yard drive with his third touchdown pass of the day, this one to Levens.

On the next series Favre takes the Pack 82 yards, to the Minnesota six. On third-and-two the call is for Favre to roll right. His first read is Levens, in the corner of the end zone; the second read is Ingram, in the back of the end zone. The third read is anyone who is open. Favre rolls right. Levens and Ingram are covered. But Bennett, whose task on this play is to simply get free wherever he can, is standing stock-still a yard deep in the end zone, waiting for Favre to see him. Eye contact is made. The ball is drilled. Touchdown.

The final score is 38–21, Green Bay. Favre's numbers for the day: 22 of 43 for 295 yards, four touchdowns and no interceptions. Chmura, with Jackson watching from the sideline, finishes with five catches for 101 yards, including a 23-yard reception on fourth down late in the fourth quarter that puts the game on ice.

"Did you see how Brett responded to every bit of pressure today?" Jordan says in the locker room. "He's our Terry Bradshaw. This is his team. He's the prankster. He's the leader. He's the man."

An hour later Favre is home. The pizza has arrived. The beer is flowing. Chmura, Winters and their wives are celebrating with guard Harry Galbreath. Brittany and a bunch of kids are playing Twister.

Favre finds a quiet room and sits for a minute. His left hip, left knee, right wrist and both elbows hurt, but his stubbly face bears the serene look of a man who has done his job well. ✦

STUBBL
PLUMMER

# SENT PACKING

BY MICHAEL SILVER

*Favre capped his first MVP season with his finest NFL performance to date, a rousing playoff upset of the reigning champion 49ers*

SI, JANUARY 15, 1996

HE KNEW IT IN HIS HEAD, IN HIS HEART AND in his aching, twisting gut, and now Mike Holmgren needed to put his mouth where his convictions were. Holmgren, the Green Bay Packers coach, had spent a week assuring his players—and anyone else who would listen—that they were capable of dethroning the Super Bowl champion San Francisco 49ers in the NFC divisional game. He and his assistants had devised a game plan so technically elegant it would make Bill Gates drool. Just before kickoff Holmgren stood in the visitors' locker room at 3Com Park, the stadium in which he launched his career as an NFL assistant, and called a motivational audible. In a move that contradicted the native San Franciscan's cerebral image, Holmgren took a deep breath and drew some magic from his mouth. ✦ "We can beat these guys, but it's not about outsmarting them or having a better scheme," he told his players. "Football is about kicking someone's ass. Football is about

V J LOVERO

LOCKED IN Favre completed 15 of his first 16 passes on the way to the victory.

physically pounding the opponent. If you want to win this game, you have to beat the crap out of these guys."

Holmgren's words struck a nerve; to the Packers it was as if Albert Einstein had turned into Al Haig. For the next three hours they dominated the heavily favored 49ers in every phase of the game to win 27–17, setting up a showdown with the Dallas Cowboys in the NFC Championship Game at Texas Stadium. If the Packers play as they did in San Francisco, they have an excellent chance to advance to their first Super Bowl in 28 years.

These Packers may not evoke memories of Vince Lombardi's roughneck teams that dominated the 1960s, but they do have some old-style machismo in their gait. That's instilled by the leadership of 34-year-old defensive end Reggie White, a spiritual man nearing the end of an arduous quest for an NFL championship, and 26-year-old quarterback Brett Favre, a country boy from Mississippi whose raunchy wit and unflappable grit have spiced up the Pack and its West Coast offense.

Despite playing with a torn left hamstring, White soared over numerous chop blocks while applying relentless pressure on 49ers quarterback Steve Young, who connected on only 32 of a playoff-record 65 passes. Favre, who this season succeeded Young as the league MVP, came through with what he acknowledged was the best game of his five-year NFL career, completing 21 of 28 passes en route to a 299-yard, two-touchdown, no-interception day.

While there were many logical explanations for the stunning outcome—beginning with Green Bay defensive coordinator Fritz Shurmur's ingenuity and extending to the offensive blueprint drawn up by Holmgren and his offensive coordinator, Sherm Lewis—the Pack also rode intangibles to this victory. "I've never been around a team quite like this," Holmgren said afterward. "I think this team is special because the players are so unselfish."

Holmgren's faith in the Packers was so great that after a 37–20 first-round win over the Atlanta Falcons, he made an uncharacteristic comment that became the talk of both the 49ers and Packers locker rooms. Asked about Green Bay's playoff prospects, Holmgren said, "We're going to win it all. Why not?" The quote quickly found the bulletin board in the San Francisco locker room. Several Niners referred to the Pack's coach as Lomas Holmgren—a reference to Detroit Lion tackle Lomas Brown, whose guarantee of a first-round victory over the Philadelphia Eagles backfired in a 58–37 Eagles win. And 49ers coach George Seifert, for whom Holmgren had served as offensive coordinator from 1989 through '91, harped on the quote in meetings.

On the other hand, the Packers carried themselves with a sly assurance in the days before the game, obviously moved by Holmgren's vote of confidence. "I'm glad he said it, because I think he believes it," Favre said. "It's time he did say it. He wouldn't have said that last year. And in the back of his mind I'll bet Coach Seifert is a little worried."

Even with an attack that was becoming more and more pass-happy, San Francisco believed it could subdue Green Bay by using the same formula it had employed in a 38–20 rout of Dallas two months earlier: Create big-play opportunities for receiver Jerry Rice and clamp down on the opposition's running game and primary receiver, in this case, Robert Brooks. But Green Bay destroyed this plan in the first quarter, which ended with the Pack leading 14–0 and embarking on another touchdown drive.

V. J. LOVERO

Brooks was targeted in a classic Favre prank—and then again in crunch time.

Though it ended with a blocked field goal, Green Bay's first possession of the game set the tone. The Packers used up seven minutes to march 48 yards, and Favre dispelled one giant misconception along the way. While watching Favre warm up before the game, some 49ers noticed his passes were fluttering and took it as a sign that he was nervous. Yeah, and Dick Clark got stage fright before *American Bandstand* tapings. "Why be nervous?" Favre asked later. "If we lose, everyone expects it. If we win, we're kings. We came to f---ing play. By the middle of the game, I was checking out cheerleaders while I was in the huddle."

Favre completed 15 of his first 16 passes, and his only two incompletions of the first half came on a throw batted down by defensive tackle Dana Stubblefield and a pass broken up by otherwise invisible All-Pro free safety Merton Hanks on an acrobatic dive. In executing the game plan to near perfection, Favre picked apart the middle of the 49ers zone, connecting with backup tight end Keith Jackson four times for 101 yards and a touchdown, including one outrageous 28-yard completion: Late in the third quarter Favre slipped as he rolled out of the pocket before zinging a perfect pass as he was regaining his balance.

In the meantime, the Green Bay defense sent a message on the 49ers' first play from scrimmage. With 7:49 left in the first quarter, Young threw an outlet pass to fullback Adam Walker, who played with a cast on his broken left thumb. Linebacker Wayne Simmons, who had the best game of his three-year career, with 12 tackles and a sack, slammed into Walker and jarred the ball loose. Rookie cornerback Craig Newsome scooped it up and ran 31 yards for the score.

Shurmur's schemes confounded the 49ers throughout the afternoon and exposed their weaknesses. The Niners could not run the ball against his creative nickel alignments—halfback Derek Loville gained five yards on eight carries—and Young's yearlong tendency to lock in on Rice became a liability. The Packers used cornerbacks Newsome and Doug Evans to bump Rice at the line, and he was double-covered on nearly every play. "Sometimes Steve stayed on Jerry too long, and that took them out of their rhythm," strong safety LeRoy Butler said. Rice still caught 11 passes for 117 yards, but most stunning was the way in which the Packers contained him after he caught the ball. After making those 11 receptions, Rice gained only 10 yards.

Having formulated defenses for 20 other games against the 49ers, Shurmur, formerly a defensive coordinator for the Los Angeles Rams and the Arizona Cardinals, knew how to disrupt the Niners' passing offense as well as anyone—and it showed. He shifted from odd- to even-numbered fronts and roughed up Young, who was intercepted twice, fumbled once and was sacked three times, by rushing players from unlikely places. Simmons, fellow linebacker Fred Strickland and Butler blitzed from all over, and on some plays 295-pound nosetackle John Jurkovic dropped into coverage.

"That was just an old-fashioned butt-kicking," said San Francisco tackle Steve Wallace. "We lived by the pass, and today we died by it. When you play an underdog and let him breathe a bit, all of a sudden he wants to tear down the house."

As much as Shurmur's game plan bewildered the 49ers—and San Francisco's first-year offensive coordinator Marc Trestman was unable to adjust—the Pack's defensive success was also a product of attitude. Early in the week Shurmur introduced 30 combinations that had many Green Bay defenders confused and bothered. On Wednesday, Holmgren went ballistic after first-team defenders repeatedly allowed scout-team receivers to find large openings. By kickoff, however, the Packers were prepared to execute Shurmur's streamlined game plan, which featured about 20 combinations.

Keeping everyone loose, as usual, was Favre, a man known as much for his bathroom humor as for his passing prowess. Like Joe Montana, Favre possesses a small-town, no-frills genuineness and a keen prankster's bent. On the Wednesday before the game his main target, Brooks, was sitting in a toilet stall when Favre heaved a cup of ice water over the top, dousing the receiver. Later that day Favre raided the locker of backup quarterback Jim McMahon and placed hot wax in McMahon's underwear.

But on the day before the game the man who had the last chuckle was Holmgren, who didn't hit the showers until every one of his players had left the locker room. With his husky jowls, soft eyes and bushy mustache, Holmgren resembles a walrus you might find in a cartoon. As he winced from the stomach pains that had plagued him all day, he showed no traces of the Lombardi-like behavior he displayed in his pregame speech. Yes, he conceded, he had told his team that football is about kicking people's asses. "But please don't use that language," he pleaded. "My mother would cringe."

Then Holmgren smiled broadly; perhaps his mom would cut him some slack this time. "I don't make guarantees," he said, "but if we play like this, I like our chances."

Why not? ✦

JOHN W. MCDONOUGH



SOAR POINT A torn hamstring didn't keep White from attacking Young (8) and Rice.

Riddell

# BITTER PILL

BY PETER KING

*Four months removed from his first MVP season, Favre revealed the gut-wrenching toll he'd paid to reach the top: an all-consuming addiction to painkillers to contend with the brutal effects of his job*

SI, MAY 27, 1996

BRETT FAVRE CAN PINPOINT WHEN, WHERE AND why he got scared straight. It happened on Feb. 27 in Room 208 of Bellin Hospital in Green Bay, where he had just undergone surgery to remove one bone spur and several bone chips from his left ankle. One minute Favre, the NFL's MVP in 1995, was talking to his girlfriend, Deanna Tynes, their seven-year-old daughter, Brittany, and a nurse. The next thing he knew, there were tubes and IVs coming out of him everywhere. ✦ He doesn't remember the 20 minutes in between, during which his limbs thrashed, his head banged backward uncontrollably, and he gnashed his teeth. During those minutes his body told him in a loud wake-up call to stop popping painkillers as if they were Lifesavers. He never heard Deanna scream to the nurse, "Get his tongue! Don't let him swallow his tongue!" He never heard a terrified Brittany ask, as she was being whisked from the room, "Is he going to die, Mom?" ✦ After the seizure had

TODD ROSENBERG

BATTLE SCARRED By '96 Favre had already endured five operations and countless hits.

ended and he had come to his senses, Favre looked into a sea of concerned medical faces and saw Packers associate team physician John Gray. "You've just suffered a seizure, Brett," Gray told him. "People can die from those."

Favre's heart sank. Upon hearing from doctors in the room that his dependence on painkillers might have contributed to the seizure, he thought, *I've got to stop the pills. I've just got to.*

During the 1995 season Favre went on such a wild ride with the prescription drug Vicodin, a narcotic-analgesic painkiller, that Deanna feared for his life. He scavenged pills from teammates. At least once he took 13 tablets in a night. But in mid-May of '96, during his final telephone call before entering the Menninger Clinic, a rehabilitation center in Topeka, Kans., to treat his dependency (and also to evaluate his occasional heavy drinking), Favre told SI that he hadn't taken Vicodin since the seizure. "I quit cold turkey," he said, "and I entered the NFL substance-abuse program voluntarily. I don't want a pill now, but I want to go into a rehab center because I want to make sure I'm totally clean. The counselors I've seen think it's best for me. The one thing they've taught me is that there will always be a spot in your brain that wants it."

A source close to Favre told SI that he initially balked at entering a rehab facility. The source said Favre also did not want to comply with a demand from his NFL-appointed addiction counselors to sign a 10-part treatment plan that called for him, among other things, to stop drinking for two years. Favre claims he doesn't have an alcohol problem. However, the league's substance-abuse policy mandates that a player who turns himself in for treatment comply with his counselors' recommendations. Had he refused to sign the treatment plan and enter a rehab center, Favre could have been considered in noncompliance with the policy. That could have triggered the penalty clause, under which he could have been subject to a four-game suspension in 1996 without pay (which would cost him $900,000). So he signed the document, revealed the depth of his problem in a press conference in Green Bay on May 14 and traveled by private jet to Kansas at 5 a.m. the next day.

The news hit hard. Favre is the newest star in the NFL galaxy, a fresh-faced 26-year-old savior with the leadership skills, charisma and Deep South backwoods likability of a Terry Bradshaw. Outside of the Dallas Cowboys' Troy Aikman and Emmitt Smith, he's probably the most significant player in football, both for what he has done on the field at a young age and for what he means to the league long-term. Many of the NFL's star quarterbacks, including John Elway, Jim Kelly, Dan Marino and Warren Moon, are in the twilight of their careers, and most of the Generation Xers—Drew Bledsoe, Trent Dilfer, Rick Mirer, Heath Shuler et al.—are struggling to make an impact. Not Favre. In the last two seasons he has thrown 71 touchdown passes, including a team-record 38 in 1995. His two-TD machine-gunning of the San Francisco 49ers in a 27–17 playoff victory last January put the Packers in the NFC Championship Game, their first title contest in 28 years, which they lost to Dallas 38–27.

But in building the longest starting streak among active quarterbacks, 68 games, Favre has paid a painful price. He has had five operations in the last six years, dating to a July 1990 car accident before his senior season at Southern Mississippi. "Brett's not coming out of the game unless a bone's sticking out," said Ty Detmer, his backup of four years in Green Bay.

VERNON J. BIEVER

Favre compelled himself to always answer the bell, no matter the cost.

Like many pro football players, Favre would—almost without thinking—take a numbing injection or a painkilling pill to get through a game. It's tough to determine the breadth of this practice, because painkillers aren't detected in annual NFL drug screenings.

"I'm sure there are a ton of NFL players out there—I mean it, a ton—who'll watch me come out and say to themselves, 'Man, that's me,' " Favre said. "That's one reason I'm talking. I hope I can help some players get help. I realize now how dangerous it is to keep using these things."

It didn't seem so dangerous to Favre when he first experienced the wonder of painkilling medication, in his seventh NFL start, on Nov. 15, 1992, against the Philadelphia Eagles. A second-year player at the time, he had separated his nonthrowing shoulder in the first quarter, and the pain was so intense that he didn't think he could go on. "I saw [backup] Don Majkowski rarin' to go, and if he'd gotten back in there, I may never have gotten my spot back," Favre said. "At halftime the doctors said, 'It's your choice, but we can shoot it up [with Novocain] without further injury.' I said, 'Let's do it.' They had to pull my shoulder out, and they stuck the needle way down in my shoulder. In a little while I didn't feel any pain. I played well, and we won the game. I thought, damn, that was easy."

He was thinking much the same thing in the wake of surgery in January 1995 to repair a herniated muscle in his right side. Doctors estimated it would take 12 months for the muscle to heal normally; Favre played a preseason game less than eight months after the surgery.

As the injuries mounted during the 1995 season, Favre began using Vicodin heavily. Seven weeks into the season, he had a throbbing turf toe, a bruised right shoulder, an arthritic right hip, a bruised left knee and a sore lower back. "I knew there

Riddell
98
4
FAVRE

was something wrong," Deanna said. "He'd ask me to ask friends for Vicodin, but I wasn't going to do that."

Favre said he believed he was hiding his addiction well, but Deanna, then Packers quarterbacks coach Steve Mariucci, and best friends and teammates Mark Chmura and Frank Winters sensed late in the season that he had a serious problem. Mariucci even told the Green Bay training staff to monitor Favre's Vicodin use. However, according to Deanna and Favre's agent, Bus Cook, in addition to the prescribed doses he received from the team, Favre also scored Vicodin from teammates who didn't finish their prescriptions and from doctors outside the organization, including one who had treated him for a past ailment. "I started finding pills everywhere," Deanna said. "I'd catch him throwing up so badly, I'd be looking for blood. And he didn't come to bed at a normal time all season long. He'd just sit there in front of the TV for hours. Sometimes I'd wake up at four o'clock and find him in front of the TV or playing solitaire on the computer. I'd say, 'What's wrong with you? You've got meetings at eight, and you haven't been to bed.' "

Despite the heavy use of painkillers, Favre was playing the best football of his life, and that complicated Deanna's efforts to get him to quit taking the pills. He was also working out like a madman with strength coach Kent Johnston. "I'm in the best shape of my life," he said in October. When Deanna would beg him to stop—she flushed down the toilet countless pills she found in his hiding places—he would reply, "Why should I stop what's helping me get through this?"

Said Chmura, Green Bay's Pro Bowl tight end, "We'd tell him time and again: 'You've got to cut this out.' But players think they're invincible, and Brett was no different. He'd be fine for the games because I think he didn't do much of it on the weekend. But some weekday nights he'd be zapped."

Deanna said she considered leaving him but worried that he might increase his Vicodin consumption if she did. Finally, at the Pro Bowl in early February, she demanded that he quit taking the pills. Favre promised he would. He didn't. At the ESPY Awards in New York on Feb. 12, she noticed that despite the fact he had not been drinking, he was slurring his words more and more as the night went on. When they returned to their hotel room, Deanna confronted Favre. "Why are you acting like this? What have you been taking?" she said.

"I took a couple of Vicodins," he said.

"A couple? No way!" she said angrily.

"Well, five or six," he said.

"How many? Tell me the truth!"

"Thirteen."

Deanna called Gray to tell him of Favre's dependency. "I was worried he was going to die," she said. Yet only after the seizure did Favre realize that getting professional help was the only way out.

BUCK MILLER

ANOTHER SHOT Playing through pain became a credo for Green Bay's battered Number 4.

For the next 2½ months Favre was on a roller coaster, confronting the addiction in sessions with his NFL-assigned counselors in Chicago and New Orleans. Deanna said Favre beat himself up emotionally. In one down moment he told her, "I may be a successful football player, but I feel like such a failure. How could I let this happen?"

"He told me he could feel we were disappointed in him," said Chmura. "He told me if it took not drinking for two years to help beat this, he'd do it. I told him, 'No problem. We'll just drink Coke with our pizza instead of Miller Lite.' "

Deanna said that all alcohol will be removed from their Green Bay house. Among other things, that means emptying the rec room refrigerator, which was stocked with only one thing: light beer.

Following Favre's revelation, NFL player after NFL player expressed sympathy for the quarterback. Favre himself said he was worried he would be cast as a drug addict if he stepped forward and admitted his problem. "I'm not blaming anyone," he said. "It's my fault. The only reason I ever did this was because I had to. *Had* to. I had to play. Injuries have cost a lot of guys their jobs in this league, and there was no way an injury was ever going to cost me my job. Then it just got out of hand."

Said Arizona Cardinals quarterback Boomer Esiason, "The worst thing in this league is getting an injury tag. I hope this opens the eyes of some players, but I doubt anyone will show the guts Brett showed in standing up there and admitting his problem."

Following his news conference Favre spent much of the night on the phone calling stunned friends. Only once in his conversation with SI did his voice dip a few octaves and show how deeply his tough outer shell has been dented. "I'm 26 years old, I just threw 38 touchdown passes in one year, and I'm the NFL MVP," he said. "People look at me and say, 'I'd love to be that guy.' But if they knew what it took to be that guy, they wouldn't love to be him, I can guarantee you that. I'm entering a treatment center tomorrow. Would they love that?"

Counselors denied Favre's request to delay reporting to rehab so he could host the first Brett Favre Celebrity Golf Tournament, in Gulfport, Miss. The event went on without him at the Windance Country Club. Deanna was there. As she sat in a golf cart under a shade tree near the 18th green, she talked about why she had hope for Favre. "A couple of years ago Brett told me he wanted to be the best quarterback in the NFL," she said. "He committed himself to it, and he did it. He'll commit himself to this. He knows his career and his life are at stake."

Deanna wiped her eyes. She took a deep breath. She sniffled a few times. "You know," she said, "he's changed already. He talks to me again. He takes Brittany and me out. He pays attention to us. A few days ago he hugged me and he thanked me for everything I've done, and he said some really nice things to me."

She wiped her eyes again. "I said, 'I can't believe it. The old Brett's back!' "

Time will tell. The true test will start in September. ✦

RICH FRISHMAN

 WAKE-UP CALL The admission that he was not invincible was Favre's first step to recovery.

PACKERS

# WARMED UP

BY PETER KING

*Favre's relationship with Packers coach Mike Holmgren began as a battle of wills, but as they prepared for their first Super Bowl, it was clear they shared both respect and a passion for winning*

SI, JANUARY 27, 1997

BRETT FAVRE SAT AT THE END OF THE GREEN BAY Packers' bench, stewing. It was the night of Oct. 20, 1994, during a game against the Minnesota Vikings at the Metrodome, and Favre seemed perilously close to losing his starting quarterback job. He had been sidelined after the first quarter by a bruised left hip, but the way he figured it the injury gave Green Bay coaches what they wanted: a convenient excuse to begin the Mark Brunell era. Though Brunell, Favre's lefthanded understudy, played well the rest of the game, Minnesota won 13–10 in overtime, dropping the underachieving Packers to 3–4. "Good," Favre recalls thinking. "We lose the rest of the games this year, that's fine with me." ✦ On the flight home, coach Mike Holmgren wouldn't make a decision on Favre's future. As is his custom, Holmgren first wanted to review the game tape and consult his coaching staff. But the statistics were telling. In 38 games directing Green Bay's passer-friendly West Coast

WALTER IOOSS JR.

WINNERS' SHARE When Favre and Holmgren found common ground, the Pack took off.

offense, the talented Favre had thrown almost as many interceptions (44) as he had touchdown passes (46). Before the season Holmgren had told Favre, "I will not hesitate to pull you if we're losing games with the same mistakes we made last year." Now Holmgren was considering benching Favre.

The next few days were dicey around Packers headquarters. In quarterbacks coach Steve Mariucci's office, Favre threw a tantrum in frustration over trying to master the complex offense. "The lowest point of his Packers career," Mariucci says. Irvin Favre, Brett's father, called Mariucci, pleading with him to have Holmgren ease up on Brett. "I know my son," Irvin says, "and if Mike hadn't stopped butchering him after he made a mistake, Brett would have dwindled to nothing." One of Holmgren's confidants, longtime friend Bob LaMonte, was certain Favre would be benched. "I know Mike was livid with Brett," LaMonte says. "Mike told me at the time that it was just galling to see a player of this magnitude continue to self-destruct."

At a coaches meeting that week, Holmgren polled each member of his offensive staff on who should be the starting quarterback. Brunell, whom the coaches considered a better decision-maker than Favre, won the vote. So what did Holmgren do? Later, he called Favre into his office and told him, "Buddy, it's your job." Holmgren's decision was based largely on his belief that Favre was close to mastering the offense and that the only thing holding him back—a tendency to force situations—was correctable. "We're joined at the hip," Holmgren told Favre. "Either we're going to the Super Bowl together, or we're going down together."

Over the next 41 regular-season games, the Packers went 30–11. Favre threw 101 touchdown passes and only 33 interceptions. He was named league MVP twice, in 1995 and '96, joining Joe Montana as the only back-to-back winners of the award. And Favre and Holmgren are going to the Super Bowl—together.

DURING A GAME, THE QUARTERBACK IS THE BRAIN OF ANY offense, and he must repeatedly make quick assessments and correct decisions. This is particularly true in the West Coast offense favored by Holmgren, who, with his expanded use of the tight end, has advanced the system created by San Diego Chargers coach Sid Gillman in the 1960s and perfected by San Francisco 49ers coach Bill Walsh in the '80s. On pass plays the quarterback may have to read three or four options in a split-second progression and then have to improvise if every option is covered.

The complexity of the system helps explain why the marriage between Holmgren and Favre was so rocky for so long. The Super Bowl will be the thoughtful Holmgren's 90th game as Packers coach, and his game plans for the first 89 contained about 1,800 plays. Favre is an act-first, think-later gunslinger who, until he reached the NFL in 1991, had never run something as elementary as the seven-on-seven passing drill. While at Southern Miss, he wowed the pro scouts with his derring-do and his cannon arm. Upon returning from a scouting trip to see Favre in '90, Buffalo Bills vice president and general manager Bill Polian was asked by owner Ralph Wilson if he had seen any good players. "I just saw the NFL's next great quarterback," said Polian.

But Favre, a second-round pick of the Atlanta Falcons, believed he would never supplant starter Chris Miller in Atlanta, and his propensity for partying got him on Falcons coach Jerry Glanville's bad side. When Favre arrived late for the team photo, Glanville fined him $1,500.

"I got trapped behind a car wreck," Favre claimed.

"You *are* a car wreck," Glanville shot back.

Nevertheless, in February 1992, new Green Bay general manager Ron Wolf dealt a first-round pick to the Falcons for Favre. As the New York Jets' director of player personnel the previous season, Wolf had been so intrigued by Favre that he wanted the Jets to draft him, but the Falcons selected him with the pick immediately ahead of New York's. Holmgren, whom Wolf had hired away from the 49ers a month before the trade, was interested in acquiring Favre, as well. "I really didn't know his reputation, but I do remember that when I'd scouted him while I was with San Francisco, I wrote in my report: 'This guy is blue-collar,' " says Holmgren. "I figured he was a throwback with a personality. And personalities as a rule don't scare me, as long as they're responsible and willing to meet me halfway."

But would Favre? He viewed Holmgren's sophisticated offense as some sort of hieroglyphics. "In the first year or so I don't think anybody on our team knew exactly what we were doing," says Favre. "I'll give you an example. We'd call Red Right, 22 Z In. I didn't care what the defense did, I was going to the Z [the flanker], and if he was covered, boom, I was gone. I was running, trying to make something happen."

It was just such a broken play that thrust Favre into the limelight. In the third game of the 1992 season, against the Cincinnati Bengals, he replaced the injured Don Majkowski and, with 13 seconds left, fired a game-winning, 35-yard touchdown pass to wideout Kitrick Taylor. "What people don't remember about that day is I should have had six or seven interceptions," says Favre. "I was all over the place." But he was also electric, and he has started every Packers game since. He finished that first season in Green Bay as a 64% passer who threw 18 touchdown passes and only 13 interceptions. But in '93 he regressed, accounting for 30 of the Pack's 34 turnovers, including 24 interceptions.

"I struggled and I struggled for a long time," Favre says. "But think about it. I got thrown into the toughest offense in the game as a starter at 22. Every other guy who's played it sat for a year or two and learned. Joe Montana sat behind Steve DeBerg. Steve Young sat behind Joe. Steve Bono sat behind both of them. Ty Detmer and Mark

Brunell sat behind me. That's why it was frustrating when people would get on me."

Throughout the 1993 season and during the first seven games of the '94 schedule, Favre was the target of Holmgren's incessant, irksome ragging. "Let the system work for you!" was one of Holmgren's nicer suggestions.

"He deserved it, believe me," Holmgren says. "He would say things to me like, 'Hey, we're 9–7, and we made the playoffs. That's a pretty good year.' And I'd say, 'You want to be 9–7 your whole life? Not me. We want to win the Super Bowl here.' We had a test of wills. He's a knucklehead. His way was simply not going to be good enough. And I don't care what his father says. If I'd treated him any differently, with more sympathy, I'd have been cheating him."

Holmgren's vote of confidence after the 1994 game in Minnesota changed Favre's perspective, but his confidence still seemed shaken. "I remember Brett so clearly in my office after the decision was made," said Mariucci, who was named 49ers coach following the 1996 season. "I told him, 'You've got two choices: You can go in the tank and feel sorry for yourself. Or you can buckle down, shake it off and be the best quarterback in football the rest of the season.' "

Upon hearing that, Favre replied, "The second half of the season is going to be like no other." He lived up to that promise. He threw only seven interceptions in the final nine games, led the Packers to the playoffs for the second consecutive season and turned his career around.

BY 1995 HOLMGREN WAS LISTENING TO FAVRE MORE AND MORE in the Saturday-morning game-plan sessions, a practice that carried over to the '96 season. On the day before a game, Holmgren, his three quarterbacks and quarterbacks coach Marty Mornhinweg discuss what will work best against that week's opponent. Holmgren asks everyone to submit, in order, their 15 favorite plays. Later, he retires to his hotel room to script Green Bay's early game plan. Holmgren hands out the First 15, as he labels the sheet, at the team meeting on the eve of the game. He'll ask Favre if he likes the order. "These are really good," Favre told Holmgren before Green Bay's 1996 NFC Championship Game against the Panthers. And he wrote Holmgren's final words to him that night on the bottom of the sheet: "Relax. Play smart."

In the early going against Carolina, Favre forced a pass on a slant route to wideout Don Beebe. Linebacker Sam Mills intercepted, setting up the touchdown that gave the Panthers a 7–0 lead. "Why'd you make that throw?" Holmgren snarled as Favre came off the field.

"Four years ago," Favre says, "I'd have been crying if he questioned me like that. I just smiled to myself, called him a name to myself and went on."

That was his last throwing error of the day. One of the plays Favre and Holmgren agreed would work against the Panthers got Green Bay even. It was play number 8 of the First 15—Two Jet All Go, Fake Fullback 40. "I will call this three times in the game," Holmgren had said in that Saturday-night team meeting, "and we will score a touchdown on one of them." Antonio Freeman was split left, with fellow wideout Andre Rison to Freeman's inside. Tight end Keith Jackson was outside the right tackle, and fullback Dorsey Levens was on the wing. At the snap all four players streaked toward the end zone.

"The Panthers play a lot of single-safety coverage in the middle of the field," Holmgren said, "and [free safety] Pat Terrell was so deep. We figured he would shade toward one of the guys, Rison or Jackson, running up the seams. Now if you run Levens out against their best corner, Eric Davis—a fullback on a great cover guy—they're not going to respect that. So Brett sees the corner keeping half an eye on the inside receiver. You can just see Davis conscious of the middle, getting a little lackadaisical on Dorsey."

Early in his career, Favre says, he might have tried to wedge a bullet to Rison or Jackson. "Now the only place I'm going to throw it is where Dorsey catches it or no one does," he says. Precisely. Levens skied over Davis to pull in the ball at the side of the end zone for a 29-yard score. Perfectly scripted, perfectly executed.

With Favre, though, not every big play is so beautiful to behold. In the third quarter, facing third-and-seven at the Carolina 32, he improvised, making a two-handed chest pass while being tackled by linebacker Kevin Greene. Favre looked for Beebe on a crossing route, but Beebe wasn't open. "I thought maybe I'd just run for it," Favre says, "but I took off and, s---, the hole closed! I started pushing Greene off as I was going down, but then I looked ahead and saw Dorsey, and I sort of pushed the ball out with my left hand just before my knees hit."

Gain of eight. First down. Holmgren just shook his head. "I thought I'd seen it all," he says.

Holmgren has seen plenty with Favre, including the inside of an addiction and dependency center. Twice during the spring of 1996 Holmgren traveled to the Menninger Clinic in Topeka, Kans., to see how Favre was getting on in his 6½-week treatment for an addiction to painkillers. "It was pretty impressive to see Mike there," Favre says. "How many bosses visit their employees in drug rehab?"

One day during his stay, Favre says, he was angered because the doctors wouldn't give him a weekend pass to be with his girlfriend (now wife), Deanna. So he punched a hole in a wall. "Mike, I've got to get out of here," Favre said during one of Holmgren's visits. "I'm going crazy. The walls are closing in on me. And I haven't thrown a football. I've got to get ready for the season."

"Don't worry," Holmgren said. "Just take care of this. The football will take of itself. You're going to be fine."

The coach knows the quarterback pretty well. ✦

4
26
HENDERSON
26

# RETURN TO GLORY

BY MICHAEL SILVER

*In Super Bowl XXXI in New Orleans, Favre and friends hit the big plays, and the Packers were NFL champs again at last*

SI, FEBRUARY 3, 1997

**IN THE HEAT OF A MOMENT THAT WILL FOREVER DEFINE** Super Bowl XXXI, Desmond Howard couldn't escape the chill of wounded pride. Even as Howard, the Green Bay Packers' nonpareil return man, raced down the Louisiana Superdome field with the New England Patriots' kickoff-coverage team in his wake, he carried a Tuna-sized chip on his shoulder. With tens of millions of viewers worldwide watching him seize the day, Howard thought only of one man—Patriots coach Bill (Tuna) Parcells—and said to himself, I can't believe he's rolling the dice and kicking me the ball. After the game Howard said, "I knew that sooner or later I was going to scorch 'em." ✦ As he reached the midpoint of his Super Bowl–record 99-yard kickoff return, Howard ran right past Parcells, who at that juncture probably had as good a chance of tackling him as anyone. But as Howard raced for the touchdown that turned a tense game into an emphatic Green Bay triumph, Parcells could only stand helplessly on the

AL TIELEMANS

CLASSIC CALL Favre's audible on the Pack's second play resulted in the TD that set the tone.

sideline and watch. For the Packers, whose 35–21 victory in Super Bowl XXXI gave the storied Green Bay franchise its first NFL championship in 29 years, that was precisely the point: After a week's worth of media coverage dominated by a 55-year-old man who craves attention the way teenage boys crave *Beverly Hills Ninja*, the game was decided by the men who play it.

Of all the big plays pulled off by the Packers this season, including long touchdown passes from quarterback Brett Favre to wideouts Andre Rison (54 yards) and Antonio Freeman (81 yards) in the Super Bowl, none was as dramatic as Howard's dash for cash. After playing for a near-minimum salary of $300,000 in 1996, Howard, a free agent, will reap huge financial rewards by becoming the first special teams player to be voted Super Bowl MVP. As he crossed the goal line with 3:10 left in the third quarter for what turned out to be the final points of the game, Howard should have been screaming, "Show me the money!" Instead, he was uncharacteristically barking at the Patriots, a team that had ticked off the Packers through the magnitude of its coach's ego. For the first time all week, Green Bay was back in the spotlight.

"This is a team that plays together, and for that reason we deserve this," said Packers tight end Keith Jackson. "Nobody is more important than anybody else, whether you're Reggie White or Brett Favre or a guy blocking on special teams. We don't get down on anyone else for making mistakes, and for that reason people don't worry about messing up. That's rare. I wish every junior high school and high school team could be around this and sniff this and sense what it's like to be a champion."

GREEN BAY'S LONG-AWAITED RETURN TO THE SUPER BOWL was an uplifting—almost hokey—story, but during the week leading up to the game it took second billing to the speculation about the Tuna's uncertain future. Give Parcells credit for two things: engineering a brilliant game plan that at one point had the Pack reeling, and sucking up more of the media's attention than any other coach in Super Bowl history. After preaching "no distractions" to his team all season, Parcells, whose contract with New England would effectively end with the final gun of the Super Bowl, thrust himself so forcefully into the public eye that he became a distraction not only to his own players but also to the Packers. "What really pisses me off is that no one gave Coach [Mike] Holmgren his due," Green Bay strong safety LeRoy Butler said Sunday night. "Everything was Parcells, Parcells, Parcells. I know Coach Parcells wants attention, but next time he should have more respect for Coach Holmgren."

The Parcells soap opera made the Packers a grumpy bunch. They had also been offended by fawning portrayals of Parcells's coaching acumen in the media and by the Patriots, and by Parcells's boast to his troops that he would "show them what to do" upon reaching the Super Bowl. The Green Bay players got so sick of reading, hearing and being asked about Parcells that Holmgren felt the need to warn them at midweek not to lose their focus. But Holmgren was also bothered by the Parcells overkill. This was clear to everyone who heard his pregame speech, during which, according to one Packer, Holmgren said, "I don't have to show you how to win this game. I've already shown you how to win. You don't need me to hold your hands. Now go out and do it."

In addition to his two touchdown passes, Favre scrambled for a score.

And they did it, to the point that another of the NFC's patented Super Blowouts appeared to be in the making midway through the first quarter: Rison's touchdown reception came on Green Bay's second play from scrimmage; New England quarterback Drew Bledsoe threw an interception on New England's ensuing possession; and just like that, the Packers led 10–0.

Though they would become the 13th consecutive AFC champion to lose in the Super Bowl, the Patriots rallied to represent their conference well. They hung tough against the Packers, who committed no turnovers and were called for only three penalties, and at one point in the first half looked capable of blowing out Green Bay.

Attacking the Packers' defense with a mixture of screens, play-action plays and rollouts, the Patriots took a 14–10 lead late in the first quarter on a pair of Bledsoe touchdown passes. "We were completely baffled," said Butler. "We were missing tackles, they were flying right past us, and they were pushing us around. No one had pushed us around all year, and they were killing us, doing stuff we hadn't seen before. It was a great game plan."

Green Bay had assumed, as had everyone else, that New England would try to control the clock by running the ball. But Parcells put this game in Bledsoe's hands from the start, and it was hard to question the strategy when New England moved at will on consecutive first-quarter scoring drives, the second touchdown having been set up by Bledsoe's 44-yard heave to rookie wideout Terry Glenn.

The Packers figured they could unnerve Bledsoe by getting an early lead and jumping on his sideline passes. However, even when Green Bay cornerback Doug Evans picked off a throw intended for Glenn on an out pattern, setting up the 37-yard Chris Jacke field goal that gave the Pack its 10–0 lead, Bledsoe stayed calm. He completed six of his next nine passes for 108 yards, including scores of one yard to fullback Keith Byars and four yards to tight end Ben Coates.

After the Coates touchdown, Green Bay defensive coordinator Fritz Shurmur called together the leaders of his unit and delivered a scolding. As Butler recalled it, Shurmur screamed to him, ends White and Sean Jones, nickelback Mike Prior and free safety Eugene Robinson, "Enough is enough! Pull your head out of your ass and go do what you're supposed to do." Then, to Butler, he added, "Go get Bledsoe. Do whatever it takes. I'll blitz you every play if I have to—just get in his face. I want him to feel you and worry about where you are all the time."

Eventually Butler and the Packers got to Bledsoe, who threw four interceptions and absorbed five sacks while completing 25 of 48 passes for 253 yards. The Patriots should have seen it coming. Anytime an offense relies on play-action passes without demonstrating a commitment to the running game, the opposing defense ultimately will stop biting on the fakes. Bledsoe threw 15 passes in the first quarter, three more than the previous Super Bowl record for passes in a first quarter (set by the San Francisco 49ers' Joe Montana in a 55–10 win over the Denver Broncos in Super Bowl XXIV), and by halftime New England had called 30 pass plays and only seven runs.

If a quarterback was to emulate Montana in this game, odds were it would be Favre, whose Super Bowl week was a sideshow second only to Parcells's. First, Favre had his life's history dissected by a wave of reporters who visited his hometown of Kiln, Miss., about an hour's drive from New Orleans. There it was learned that when Brett was a kid, the family dog had been eaten by an alligator, that Brett had preferred to sleep on top of his sheets as a child so that he wouldn't have to make his bed and that he had gastrointestinal powers, said his college roommate, "that could bring tears to your eyes." Then on the Tuesday of Super Bowl week a story broke in the *Green Bay Press-Gazette* that Favre, who spent more than six weeks in a rehab facility in the spring of 1996 for addiction to a painkiller, would no longer be tested by the NFL for alcohol as part of his aftercare program. With Bourbon Street beckoning, this was big news—until the report turned out to be false.

The irony was that as this talk of his resuming drinking was going down, the flu-plagued Favre could barely handle chicken soup. He spent the Thursday night before the game in his hotel room, shivering under his covers with a 101° temperature. "I was worried," he admitted late on Sunday. "I'd waited my whole life to play in this game, and now I wasn't going to be healthy. But the night before the game I slept great. I fell asleep at 9:30 with the TV clicker in my hand, and I felt pretty good when I woke up. But I was nervous before kickoff, and I kept dry-heaving all game."

Favre was clear-headed enough to burn New England for two touchdowns after making adjustments at the line of scrimmage. On the first he detected that the Patriots, with both their safeties up at the line, were about to come with an all-out blitz. Earlier on Sunday, while watching Super Bowl XXIV highlights in his hotel room, Favre had seen Montana audible in a nearly identical situation. So Favre changed the play from

322 Y Stick, a safe quick-out to tight end Mark Chmura, to 74 Razor, which called for Rison to run a deep post route. It wasn't the smoothest switch—in the middle of the audible Favre yelled "Oh, s---!" before finally barking out the signal for 74 razor—but it worked perfectly. Rison turned cornerback Otis Smith around and was open by about five yards when he caught Favre's pass at the 20. Rison duckwalked the last few yards to the end zone.

After New England had taken its 14–10 lead, Favre, who would complete 14 of 27 passes for 246 yards, put Green Bay ahead for good with another astute call. Less than one minute into the second quarter, he saw the Patriots' defensive backs line up in single coverage against a three-wideout set, with strong safety Lawyer Milloy on Freeman, the slot receiver. "A safety on me, playing bump-and-run?" Freeman said incredulously after the game. "I liked my chances." Sensing that the Patriots were going to blitz again, Favre audibled to a blocking scheme that was designed to give him maximum protection, then found Freeman down the right sideline. Freeman easily outran Milloy and free safety Willie Clay for an 81-yard score, the longest touchdown from scrimmage in Super Bowl history.

Green Bay added 10 more points to take a 27–14 halftime lead, and it looked as if New England was done. In fact most of the Packers were surprised the Patriots had hung around that long. Consider what took place during a Green Bay team meeting on Thursday: Upon being cautioned by Holmgren to compliment New England in media interviews, outside linebacker Wayne Simmons finally snapped, "I'm tired of saying how great this team is. I've been watching them on film, and they look like crap." Other players grunted in agreement until, according to one Packer, Holmgren said, "Wayne, I appreciate your restraint. To tell you the truth, I agree with you. Believe me, I'd like to tell the world I'm going to kick Parcells's ass too."

THE PACKERS VIEWED PARCELLS AS TOO EAGER FOR MEDIA attention. They bristled when Parcells's agent, Robert Fraley, leaked a story that Parcells would leave New England after the Super Bowl because of his rift with Robert Kraft. The Packers were further annoyed when Kraft and Parcells made a mock announcement at a midweek press conference that Parcells had been signed to a 10-year contract to manage the Kraft family's paper mill. The joke landed flat. "Parcells jinxed his team by starting all that s---," Butler said while stewing in his hotel room last Friday night. "Mike [Holmgren] is really pissed."

Howard was a tad angry as well. Given his three punt returns for touchdowns during the regular season and his pivotal performance (two long punt returns, one for a score) against the 49ers in Green Bay's divisional playoff victory, he felt the Patriots shouldn't have been so vocal during the week about their intentions to kick to him.

Howard broke free for 32 yards on his first punt return, setting up the game's initial touchdown, and helped facilitate a second-quarter field goal with a 34-yard runback of a punt. Still, the New England players were barking at him, saying, "Nothing for you today, baby. We going to shut you down," and Howard returned their affection. "I have never, ever talked so much during a game," he said later, his hoarse voice the proof.

Howard said he told Favre at halftime, "I'm going to take one of these kicks back; it's only a matter of time." He struck at the perfect time, after the Patriots had cut the Pack's lead to 27–21 on a seven-play, 53-yard touchdown drive that culminated in halfback Curtis Martin's 18-yard run.

Cognizant of New England's tendency to kick the ball to the opponent's right side, Green Bay's coaches for this game had switched Howard from the left side to the right for the first time all season. He caught the ball at the one, burst up the middle and swept through the Patriots' coverage for his first kickoff return for a touchdown as a pro. "We were feeling good before that," Clay said, "and then Desmond Howard broke our backs." Green Bay was up by two touchdowns. New England still had lots of time, but the Packers' defense clamped down, as White got all three of his sacks in the final 18 minutes.

After the game Howard, who finished with a Super Bowl–record total of 244 return yards, and his agent, Leigh Steinberg, shared a limousine ride from the Superdome to the Packers' hotel with a representative from Disney, who discussed a TV commercial and a parade appearance. Chewing nervously on the wrapper of a huge victory cigar, Howard listened as Steinberg filled him in on offers to appear on Leno and Letterman. Then Howard worried aloud about shipping a new car he had recently purchased from Green Bay to his home in Boca Raton, Fla., until the Disney rep interrupted. "Uh, Desmond," he said, "I think after tonight you can afford to have your car shipped just about anywhere you want it, as many times as you want."

Upon reaching the hotel Howard was whisked into a service elevator and up to his room. Eventually he made it back downstairs to the Packers' victory party, a raucous affair from which Favre sought temporary refuge in a nearby stairwell. There Favre reflected upon his tumultuous off-season, which included the death of his best friend, Mark Haverty, in a car accident in which Brett's brother, Scott, was driving.

"Through everything," Brett said, "I really believed I'd be here today." He laughed and continued, "Right here in this stairwell, talking about being world champions. My best friend's gone forever. Trouble never seems to be far away, and the future won't be all rosy, but they can't take this away from me. Thirty years from now, the kids will be getting ready for Super Bowl LXI, and NFL Films will drag out Steve Sabol—he'll be around 102 then—and he'll talk about how Brett Favre fought through such adversity. And there will be other players and coaches. But I know this: We etched our place in history today." ✦

AL TIELEMANS

 NAILED IT Howard's kick-return TD clinched Green Bay's first title in nearly three decades.

81

# SECOND TO NONE

BY MICHAEL SILVER

*In yet another showdown with San Francisco, Mike Holmgren gave Favre free rein, and he passed the Pack to a second straight NFC title*

SI, JANUARY 19, 1998

**THEY ARE THE YIN AND YANG OF THE CHEESEHEAD** Nation, one spewing smoke from his ears, the other playfully kicking up dust. While coach Mike Holmgren does his best to stomp the fun out of the Green Bay Packers' drive for a second consecutive championship, All-Pro quarterback Brett Favre is setting off stink bombs. Forgive the rest of the Packers if they're a bit bewildered by the conflicting demeanors of their two leaders. Holmgren and Favre make Ted Kaczynski and Tara Lipinski seem compatible. ✦ Holmgren may be one of the NFL's biggest control freaks, but he's smart enough to know who rules the football universe. In a driving rainstorm at San Francisco's 3Com Park, Holmgren put Green Bay's NFC championship hopes in Favre's hands, and Favre flawlessly delivered a 23–10 victory over the 49ers. Watching the three-time MVP shred the Niners' defense—the league's top-ranked unit in 1997—had to be disconcerting for the AFC champion Denver Broncos,

WALTER IOOSS JR.

STRIPPED FOR ACTION A repeat Super Bowl appearance awaited after the 49ers were bested.

who gave up 41 points the last time they faced Favre, late in the '96 season. For when Green Bay and Denver meet in Super Bowl XXXII, John Elway, scarily enough, will be the second most dangerous quarterback on the field.

Neither nerves nor blitzes nor the elements have been able to slow Favre's march to San Diego, and unless the Broncos can come up with something quick—handcuffs? itching powder in Favre's jock?—they'll be hard-pressed to avoid another AFC wash-out in the Super Bowl. After tearing up San Francisco with 222 passing yards in a game the Pack was never in danger of losing, Favre conceded that the prospect of facing a team coached by his close friend and former mentor, Steve Mariucci, had made him uncharacteristically jumpy. "I was real nervous last night," he said while scarfing a spicy postgame hot dog in the nearly deserted Green Bay locker room. "I said more prayers before this game than before any game I ever remember. No formal prayers, but just praying for, well, wisdom, I guess. We were playing a great team with a great defense, and I just prayed that I'd play smart and make good decisions."

On the night before the game, Holmgren had made the best decision of all: unveiling a strategy that entrusted Favre with killing the Niners' spirit. Holmgren, who scripts the Pack's first 15 plays, typically calls for no more than eight passes in that stretch. This time he distributed a sheet to his players calling for nine passes—the most pass-happy plan Favre remembers receiving during his six seasons as Green Bay's quarterback.

As it turned out, this was the best script since *Sling Blade*. When Favre is on his game, as he was in this one, it's the defensive backs who should be saying prayers, and Denver corners Darrien Gordon and Ray Crockett undoubtedly will be doing so in the days ahead. Like Detroit Lions halfback Barry Sanders, with whom he shared this year's league MVP award, Favre can humiliate a defender on any play.

Throwing quickly and with amazing accuracy, Favre went right after San Francisco cornerbacks Rod Woodson and Marquez Pope, often connecting on slant routes the two have seen thousands of times in practice and on film. The corners knew what was coming, but they were powerless to stop it. The 49ers were determined to gang up on Pro Bowl halfback Dorsey Levens and stop the run early, leaving Woodson and Pope in single coverage on wideouts Robert Brooks and Antonio Freeman. Favre's precision was such that his receivers needed only to create the slightest opening. Gordon and Crockett have had success playing aggressively of late, but unless the Broncos can find a way to get to Favre as soon as the ball is snapped, they'll be faced with a similar dilemma. "We came out with the attitude that they had to adjust to our scheme, rather than us changing for them," Packers fullback William Henderson said after Sunday's game. "When we have all our weapons in use like we did today, and Brett is rolling, it's going to be hard for anyone to stop us."

Green Bay marched 68 yards on its first six plays. Four of them were passes by Favre, and the count didn't include a play that drew a 24-yard interference penalty against Woodson. The Packers settled for a 19-yard Ryan Longwell field goal, but the tone had been set. "I think their defensive players were rattled by that first drive," said Ross Verba, the Packers' rookie left tackle. "You could see it in their eyes."

Favre went for the kill early in the second quarter, two plays after Green Bay free safety Eugene Robinson had intercepted a pass by Steve Young and returned it 58 yards to the San Francisco 28. The Packers sent three receivers to the right side and split Freeman left. Freeman's quick inside slant spun Pope in a circle, and Freeman crowed afterward, "I treated him like a freak; I turned him out." Favre delivered a crisp pass at the 20, and the wideout raced past three flailing defenders for a touchdown and a 10–0 Green Bay lead. This was the Pack's 14th offensive play and ninth pass, and the 49ers defenders were shaking their heads and quoting Busta Rhymes, wondering: What the deally yo?

The Niners had adopted a regression-therapy approach to stopping Favre, reasoning that by shutting down Levens early and pressing Favre's receivers they could make him revert to the wild, reckless quarterback who once threw 24 interceptions in a season. But Holmgren seems to have tamed this pony. In the second half Favre showed his maturity by allowing Levens to grind out yards—he had 71 of his 114 after halftime—and drain the clock as the rain came pouring down. Favre, who completed 16 of 27 passes, called an audible on only four or five plays, even though he probably could have feasted on the 49ers secondary. While Young had some tenuous moments throwing into the wind, Favre simply generated his own gusts. "The difference in this game was arm strength," said LeRoy Butler, Green Bay's Pro Bowl strong safety. "Steve threw into the wind; Brett threw through the wind."

Six days before the game Butler had told Favre, "Don't worry if you turn it over. Our defense will win it. The burden is on us." Favre glared back and said, "No, no, no—I'm going to get that s--- done." Both were right. The Niners, supremely confident they could run the ball against the Packers, went nowhere. Mariucci benched halfback Garrison Hearst, coming off a broken left collarbone that had sidelined him for four games, after he gained only 12 yards on eight first-half carries; Hearst's replacement, Terry Kirby, ran six times for 21 yards. Green Bay frustrated San Francisco's blockers with inside stunts and new blitzes featuring Butler on the weak side.

The Niners threw their share of blitzes at Favre, and he read them expertly. "It's hard to blitz him," 49ers strong safety Tim McDonald had said earlier in the week, "because the guy is so tuned in, he picks it up before the snap."

Recognition was rampant for both teams—no surprise, given the numerous close ties between them. While Favre and Mariucci, who from 1992 to '95 was the quarterbacks coach in Green Bay, made the best of an awkward situation, Holmgren was grouchy even by his lofty standards. He prohibited his players from receiving calls in their hotel rooms and barked at players to stop making phone calls to Mariucci.

Some players call Holmgren Mussolini; Favre is more like Federico Fellini. During the Pack's 21–7 divisional playoff victory over the Tampa Bay Buccaneers, Bucs defensive tackle Warren Sapp got in Favre's face after one hard rush and said, "I'm going to be after your ass all day." Favre patted the 288-pound Sapp on the gut and said, "With that tummy, I don't think you're going to make it." On Saturday, as he concluded a production meeting with Fox announcers, Favre set off a stink bomb. "John Madden had some sort of adverse reaction," Favre said. "He was bracing himself against the wall, looking ill."

Yet Holmgren was in his element on Sunday as he delivered a fiery pregame speech, telling the Packers to "go for the jugular . . . dominate . . . kick their ass." Butler says Holmgren "was turning red. You could just feel the heat wave." Favre, meanwhile, played it cool, asking teammates as they rode the bus to the stadium, "Hey, guys, what do you say we kick some ass?"

With two weeks to prepare for the Broncos, Favre and Holmgren undoubtedly will be more polarized than ever in their approaches. Maybe their good cop/bad cop routine is by design. Says Verba, "Asses were tight this week, but Brett Favre is the leader of the Pack when it comes down to it. He keeps us loose."

But as much as some Green Bay players bitch about Holmgren's overbearing authority, they love having him on their sideline come Sunday. "Mike is the smartest coach in the league," Butler says. "The only coach who should be compared with him is dead, and that's Lombardi."

The next test for Favre is against Elway, who sat out the teams' last meeting, a 41–6 Green Bay victory that came after Denver had already clinched home field advantage throughout the AFC playoffs. "It's stupid to bring that one up," Favre says. "It'll be great to go into a big game against John. He's probably the quarterback I'm closest to among the guys who've been around for a while. We play alike, I think. I patterned my game after his. I admire him so much—the way he plays, the way he carries himself."

Ah, Brett, the paragon of decorum. While waiting for his hot dog in the Packers locker room on Sunday, Favre, 28 going on 12, dispensed some advice to Mariucci's 11-year-old son, Adam. "Smell this," Favre urged, offering a tiny vial of yellow liquid. Adam complied and recoiled; the liquid had the scent of rotten eggs. "Here's what you do," Favre said, handing the boy the vial. "Take this to school tomorrow. And at recess, put one drop somewhere and see what people do. One drop'll kill 'em."

It's a game plan Holmgren would hate, but one to which the coach could probably relate. One dose of Favre can be too much for opponents to take. ✦

PETER READ MILLER

 SLIPPING AWAY San Fran game-planned to shut down Levens, but the strategy backfired.

25
25

# ONE PLAY

BY PETER KING

*Forty heart-pounding Super Bowl seconds underscored the complexities and snap decisions that went into a Brett Favre touchdown pass*

SI, AUGUST 17, 1998

**IN THE METICULOUSLY TIME-MANAGED WORLD OF THE** NFL, in which months of off-season preparation are followed by weeks of training camp and then a daily regimen leading up to each game, the culmination of all that planning is compressed into 40-second segments. That's the amount of time allotted between the end of one play and the start of the next. Here's a stop-action account of one play in the life of the Packers' offense, as seen through the eyes of three-time league MVP Brett Favre. It's Green Bay's ball, first-and-10 at the Denver 22, with about 11 minutes left in the first quarter of a scoreless Super Bowl XXXII. The play clock behind each end zone resets to .... ✦ **:40** After landing hard at the end of a 13-yard catch, Packers wideout Antonio Freeman rises and shakes out the cobwebs. Green Bay coach Mike Holmgren stares at the field, looking to see where the ball will be spotted. ✦ **:38** Favre strides upfield, looking to the sideline for Andy Reid, his quarterbacks coach. Reid, who's wearing a headset, relays the

V.J. LOVERO

MIND GAME Favre misread the Denver D at first but still got the pass away to Freeman.

plays from Holmgren to the quarterback by way of a tiny speaker in Favre's helmet.
**:37** Once he knows the down and distance, Holmgren begins seven seconds of decision-making, determining which one of the 120 plays on his plastic-coated game plan is the best for this situation. All week he spoke to Favre about stretching the red zone a few yards; the Broncos have allowed a generous 65% completion rate between the 15 and 20 all season. Holmgren could also run Dorsey Levens, who has shredded the Denver defense for 28 yards on his first four carries. Even if Green Bay lines up three or four wideouts, Denver must respect the run.
**:34** Reid pushes the red button on his right hip, opening communications with Favre. "First-and-10 at the plus-22," Reid says. "Think red zone." Favre is excited. He thinks Holmgren is going to call a pass.
**:30** "Two Jet All Go," Holmgren says, speaking into his mike to Reid. The Packers will go for the touchdown. Four wideouts will spread across the field and streak toward the end zone.
**:29** The Packers make two substitutions: wide receivers Derrick Mayes and Terry Mickens for fullback William Henderson and tight end Mark Chmura.
**:28** "Two Jet All Go," Favre hears in his helmet. Reid then tells him the formation—"Spread Right"—but Favre already knows it. It's the only formation Holmgren would use with Two Jet All Go.
**:25** "Spread Right, Two Jet All Go, on one," Favre says in the huddle. As the players break, Freeman looks to Mayes, who will line up outside him, on the far right, and says, "Remember to keep our spacing right."
**:24** The four wide receivers move to their positions: Robert Brooks split wide left, a step off the line of scrimmage; Mickens on the line, three paces outside of left tackle Ross Verba; Freeman in the right slot; Mayes split wide. The only player in the backfield with Favre is Levens, who excels at picking up blitzes.
**:19** Favre cranes to see the play clock. Good, he thinks, plenty of time. Next he starts looking over the defense as he settles in at the line.
**:15** Favre is on his own now. Electronic communication between the bench and the quarterback, introduced exclusively for play-calling, is cut at the 15-second mark by an NFL official in the press box.
**:14** Most quarterbacks check the safeties first for clues to the defense's plans. Favre is no different. Broncos safeties Steve Atwater and Tyrone Braxton are 12 yards off the line. Even with the four-wideout set, neither appears to be cheating toward any receiver or to be thinking blitz. Zone coverage more than likely, Favre reasons.
**:13** The cornerbacks are five and 10 yards off the line. They're giving up the under-

neath ball, Favre thinks, but there's no reason to call an audible. He likes the play.

**:12** As he stands behind center Frank Winters, Favre guesses that the anxious-looking outside linebacker to his left, John Mobley, will blitz. That means Favre must change the blocking assignment for Levens, who in Two Jet was to have picked up any blitzer coming from the right side.

**:11** Favre turns and shouts to Levens, "Three Jet! Change to Three Jet!" Levens now knows to look for any blitzer coming from his left.

**:09** Now Favre barks the count, "Three 19! Three 19! Set! Hut!"

**:08** The ball is snapped. Favre's right leg drives backward as he begins a five-step drop. (The play clock is turned off at the snap, but here is a second-by-second account as the play unfolds.)

**:07** Two steps into his drop, Favre glances left and sees Brooks and Mickens running into traffic. Mobley drops to cover Mickens, so Favre thinks Freeman or Mayes might be open on the right before Atwater, lined up on the left, can get across the field. On the third step, Favre's head swivels slightly right. Mayday!

**:06** Out of the corner of his right eye Favre sees number 39, cornerback Ray Crockett, steaming in. Four steps into his drop all Favre can see is that 39 getting bigger and bigger. Favre knows he'll get hit, because Levens is helping Winters pick up blitzing linebacker Bill Romanowski. ("I blew it," Favre thinks of his changing Levens's blocking assignment.)

**:05** As he takes the fifth step and plants, Favre looks past Crockett while cocking his arm. He sees Braxton crouch, as though he's expecting Freeman to run a quick hook or out. Bad move, Favre thinks. But it makes sense: Braxton knows Crockett is blitzing. That leaves an open area in the middle of the field, so Braxton figures Favre will surely dump the ball there before he gets smacked.

**:04** Get rid of it quick, is all Favre is thinking now. Freeman accelerates past Braxton. Favre figures Freeman will beat Braxton to the back of the end zone, so he aims for the end line. Standing on the Denver 29, he throws a perfect 39-yard spiral.

**:03** Crockett gives Favre a shove, not the jarring shot the quarterback expected to receive.

**:02** Behind Braxton now, Freeman looks over his left shoulder and sees the pass coming. Out of the corner of his eye he also sees Atwater closing fast from the left. "Like a freight train," Freeman says later.

**:01** The ball nestles into Freeman's hands, and as he plants his right foot just inside the end line, Atwater delivers a wicked shot with his right forearm to Freeman's left shoulder. Too late. For the 38th time in five months, Favre thrusts two fists into the air to celebrate a touchdown pass. "No feeling in the world like it," he says later. ✦

4

# FINEST HOUR

BY PETER KING

*Facing the best defense he said he'd ever seen, Favre reached deep and produced yet another memorable performance*

SI, OCTOBER 22, 2001

AFTER THE PACKERS' FINAL PRACTICE OF the week, Brett Favre drove 30 miles in a steady rain to a 1,000-acre hunting preserve in northeast Wisconsin. He climbed a tree and sat in a stand with his bow and arrows, waiting for a buck. The rain never let up, and Favre sat for four hours without firing a single arrow. On Sunday morning he was still so eager to shoot that before he left for Lambeau Field and Green Bay's showdown with the Super Bowl champion Baltimore Ravens, he fired three arrows at a target in his backyard. "All three were dead center in the bull's-eye," Favre said on Sunday night. "I didn't think anything of it at the time, but I guess it was a good omen." ✦ Favre, 32, has won three league MVPs and one Super Bowl. He has passed for more than 4,000 yards three times and thrown at least 30 touchdown passes five times. Last week, in his 150th NFL game, going against what he called the best defense he's ever faced, he played

HARRY HOW/GETTY IMAGES

RIDING HIGH Favre had reason to celebrate as he carved up a vaunted Ravens D.

arguably the best game of his life. "I'd be hard-pressed to say, considering the quality of the team we played, that I've ever had a better game," he said.

In Green Bay's stunning 31–23 win, Favre had the most efficient passing day by a Ravens' opponent since 1997 (27 completions in 34 attempts, for 79%), accounting for 337 yards and three touchdowns with no interceptions. Favre led the four longest touchdown drives allowed by Baltimore this year (59, 74, 80 and 82 yards), keeping the Ravens on their heels by using a quirky mix of play-action passes and runs out of the shotgun.

"I'm not in fear of anyone," Favre said from his home four hours after the game ended, while an outdoors show played on the TV. "But I watched six Baltimore games on tape. I saw that so many teams have chances but never capitalize. When [offensive coordinator] Tom Rossley talked to our offense about the game last week, he told us we could have 400 yards if we executed right. I'm looking around the room at our young guys, and I can see them thinking, Sure. Who's he trying to kid?"

The Ravens, who haven't permitted an opposing player to run for 100 yards in 38 games, line up mountainous tackles Sam Adams and Tony Siragusa to plug the middle. Outside speed rushers Michael McCrary and Peter Boulware chase quarterbacks relentlessly, while ace cover cornerbacks Chris McAlister and Duane Starks blanket receivers. For insurance, there's pit-bull middle linebacker Ray Lewis.

Everyone has tried to get Baltimore off-balance by spreading out and adding extra receivers to get the 340-pound Siragusa off the field. Rossley thought if he put Favre in the shotgun most of the day but ran out of it often, he'd keep the defense honest and not let the pass rushers cut loose. Rossley calls the plays snapped out of the shotgun "keeps." Said Favre, "They'd think it was a run when we had two backs beside me, and sometimes it was. After the game McCrary came up to me and said, 'I played the keeps all day.' "

Precision was vital too, because the Ravens don't leave much room for receivers to breathe. In the third quarter, with Green Bay leading 17–10, Favre sent Donald Driver and two other receivers down the left side, while Antonio Freeman did a curl on the right. He stared a hole in Freeman, trying to make the safety cheat, all the while yearning to throw deep to Driver. "From the time I started playing quarterback in the fifth grade," Favre said, "I was always taught not to throw a pass when the safety is there to help. But I thought that I could get this ball in to Donald. Before he turned for it, I threw the ball as hard as I could, and the safety charged. The ball got to Donald at the perfect time." The 37-yard completion helped set up Green Bay's third touchdown.

Afterward the Favres—Brett, wife Deanna and daughters Brittany and Breleigh—joined a crowd of players and their families at Brett's Green Bay steak house for dinner. A fan asked the quarterback if the Ravens had talked much trash. "Not at all," Favre said. "They were the classiest guys we've played. I talked with a bunch of them after the game—McCrary, Goose, Lewis—and they said, 'Great job. Stay healthy. Hope we meet in the Super Bowl.' " ✦

KIRK WAGNER/THE POST-CRESCENT

 GROUND DOWN While Ahman Green found the going tough, his QB passed for three scores.

SIRAGUSA
WAHLE
RAVENS

Riddell
55

# LEADER OF THE PACK

BY MICHAEL SILVER

*A renewed enthusiasm and some new weapons on offense had Brett and the boys set up for another solid run toward the postseason*

SI, NOVEMBER 18, 2002

BRETT FAVRE LOCKED IN ON HIS TARGET AND barreled into the fray. *Man, it's been a long time since I've done this,* the Green Bay Packers' ebullient quarterback thought as he charged across the wet Lambeau Field grass on Sunday, his fragile left knee be damned. Wideout Terry Glenn had just turned a short Favre pass into an apparent 47-yard touchdown, and the quarterback was intent on reaching Glenn before the receiver could make his first Lambeau Leap into the stands. As Favre raced frantically to the end zone, he looked like the victim of one of his own classic pranks, a man with hot sauce in his jock. When, finally, he slammed Glenn to the ground and rolled underneath him, Favre screamed, "That's why we brought your ass in here!" ✦ Never mind that after a replay review, Glenn was ruled to have been down at the one-yard line or that Favre sheepishly admitted to Green Bay coach Mike Sherman after the game, "That was the only time I felt any knee pain all day." Favre's brilliance has always included a

HARRY HOW/GETTY IMAGES

ON TARGET In the midst of a 12–4 season, the Green and Gold's QB was typically driven.

measure of recklessness, and this was a 33-year-old living legend at his finest—decisive, unpretentious and willing to embrace the emotion of the moment.

"When something like that happens—and we had a lot of moments like that today—you feel so powerful as a quarterback," Favre said after the Packers had spanked the Lions 40–14 for their seventh consecutive victory, the franchise's longest winning streak since 1963. "You feel like you can make any throw or hand off to whomever and something great is going to take place. I don't know where we're going to end up, but it's impressive what we've been able to do so far, and it sure has been a lot of fun."

When Favre has this much fun, football fans get goose bumps—and the rest of the NFL feels the chill. With a league-best 8–1 record, Green Bay has the inside track for home field advantage throughout the NFC playoffs, evoking memories of the 1996 season, when Favre won his only Super Bowl. Considering the team's 11–0 postseason record at Lambeau and Favre's 32–0 record in home games when the temperature at kickoff is 34° or colder, it's not hard to predict who will have the psychological edge if the road to the Super Bowl crosses frozen tundra.

"I know what it's like to go there in January, and it's not a pleasant experience," says Lions free safety Eric Davis, who, as a member of the Carolina Panthers in the '96 NFC Championship Game, suffered a 30–13 defeat in 3° weather at Lambeau. "If you're not acclimated to that weather, your body doesn't know how to respond, and your fast-twitch muscles shut down. Everybody in the league has a scary image of Green Bay in January."

In this unpredictable NFL season the race for home field is far from over, especially when you consider that the Pack's remaining schedule includes road games against the Tampa Bay Buccaneers and the San Francisco 49ers, two of the NFC's three 7–2 teams. (The other, the New Orleans Saints, handed Green Bay its only loss, 35–20, on Sept. 15.) All we know for sure is that Green Bay owns a five-game division lead over the second-place Lions with seven to play and is well on its way to winning the inaugural NFC North title.

After being shredded by Favre (26 of 39, 351 yards, two touchdowns in less than three quarters of work) on Sunday, Davis and the rest of the Lions left Titletown as believers. "They're f------ good," Davis said late on Sunday from his suburban Detroit apartment. "They're smart and efficient on offense, their defense makes you pay for every mistake, and they know they have a future first-ballot Hall of Fame quarterback who will give them a chance to win every game. They're borderline cocky, and that's what you have to be to be great."

In his 12th season, Favre shows no sign of decline. In fact, if his knee holds up, the NFL's only three-time MVP could add a fourth. His garish 2002 numbers include a 65.7 completion percentage, a 17–4 touchdown-to-interception differential and a 101.7 passer rating. "I don't think Brett would admit to this," Sherman says, "but he's at a

JOHN BIEVER

Glenn proved a valuable addition to the '02 wideout corps, catching 56 passes for 817 yards.

level he hasn't been at before. For one thing, whereas in past years he's led by example, now he's more apt to let his leadership be known."

Making speeches does not come naturally to Favre. "I'm not a very vocal person," he insists. "As outgoing and inclined to have fun as I am, I backpedal when it's time to talk to the team, and I have a hard time saying the right things or believing that what I say makes a difference. Then again, there are guys who say all the right things, and then they step on the field and aren't worth a darn."

Like Joe Montana, the man he passed early the Lions game to move into sixth place on the NFL's career passing yardage list, Favre is a homespun hero who uses levity to lead. "I'm 100 percent convinced that all people, at any job, are at their best when they're relaxed," he says. Thus the Pack's merry prankster, who once tormented teammates by dousing them with cold water as they sat on the toilet, is now expanding his repertoire. "The new thing is doe urine," says backup quarterback Doug Pederson, Favre's frequent hunting buddy. "I got a case of it sent to me, and Brett soaked some into a sock and put it in [guard] Marco Rivera's locker. Man, was it rank."

Four games into the season some observers were saying the same thing about the Packers, whose Week 2 loss to the Saints came amidst narrow victories over the

Atlanta Falcons, the Lions and the Panthers. A players-only meeting after the loss energized the defense, which has forced at least two turnovers in every game during the winning streak. "We talked about how we needed to stop buying into our hype and questioning the coaches' calls, and just play to our level," recalls free safety Darren Sharper, the team's defensive leader. "From then on we started smacking people in practice, just full-out tackling guys."

There were obvious exceptions, of course. "You hit Number 4," Sharper says, "and you get a box lunch and a road map out of town." This became especially true after the Packers saw their season flash before their eyes during a 30–9 victory over the Washington Redskins on Oct. 20, when Favre sprained the lateral collateral ligament in his left knee on a third-quarter hit by linebacker LaVar Arrington. Favre feared his career was over—*I never thought it would end like this*, he thought when he heard the pop in his knee—but after Green Bay's bye week he returned for a Monday night game against the Miami Dolphins to extend his record streak of consecutive starts by a quarterback (166 and counting) and said on Sunday that he's "close to 100 percent."

As long as Favre stays healthy, his teammates believe they can withstand any hardship, such as when Lions linebacker Chris Claiborne knocked Pro Bowl halfback Ahman Green (mild concussion) out of the game with a resounding hit midway through the second quarter. The Green Bay offense kept on rolling, because Favre has plenty of other playmakers in his arsenal, including a most unlikely star—fourth-year wideout Donald Driver. In his first three seasons Driver caught a total of 37 passes, including 13 for 167 yards last year while playing behind Antonio Freeman, Bill Schroeder and Corey Bradford, all of whom have since departed. On Sunday, Driver had 11 receptions for 130 yards. "I don't want to say I knew he was that good," Favre says, "but I knew he'd give effort that was beyond belief. I wish there were 52 other guys on this team just like him."

Driver's effort was apparent on the play of the day: that pass from Favre to Glenn on a quick slant from the Detroit 47 with 31 seconds left in the first half and Green Bay up 23–7. Glenn—whose erratic behavior led the New England Patriots to trade him to Green Bay last March—beat bump-and-run coverage from Chris Cash, made the catch and raced to the left sideline; Driver sprung him loose by sealing off Davis at the 25.

Long after the game, as he sat in a room in Lambeau flipping a half-full water bottle into the air, Favre remained giddy about Glenn's big play, which set up Najeh Davenport's one-yard touchdown run. "I've always been confident," Favre said, "but this is the most confident I've ever been, and the reason is the way the guys around me are playing. Donald made a great block, and Glenn made the guy covering him look silly."

Take that last point as gospel. Favre happens to be an expert on the subject. ✦

JOHN BIEVER

 AHH, MAN Green rushed for 1,240 yards in '02, his third of five straight 1,000-yard seasons.

PACKERS
30

# DO YOU BELIEVE?

BY PETER KING

*His father's death weighing heavily on him in the 2003 season, Brett did what Big Irv had raised him to do—play his heart out*

SI, JANUARY 12, 2004

THE HOME STRETCH OF THE 2003 SEASON HAS taken Brett Favre's breath away. First there was the emotional toll, after his father died suddenly, four days before Christmas, at the age of 58. Then there was the divine intervention, when the Arizona Cardinals' 25-yard touchdown pass on their final play of the season knocked the Minnesota Vikings out of the playoffs and put Favre's Green Bay Packers in. Finally, there was the physical pounding. On Sunday, an hour after the Packers' heart-stopping 33–27 overtime win against the Seattle Seahawks in the NFC wild-card game at Lambeau Field, Favre was moving gingerly through the players' lounge. ✦ "I don't know how much more of this I can take," he said. "It's killing me." ✦ "The emotion of it all?" he was asked. ✦ "That," Favre said, grimacing as he sat, "and I can hardly breathe. Got nailed in the ribs really bad today. [Seattle defensive end] Chike Okeafor leveled me." ✦ "Say anything to him?" Favre was asked.

PETER READ MILLER

PAY DIRT Favre and Franks reveled in their playoff touchdown against the Seahawks.

"Yeah," he said with a wry smile. "I went up to him and said, 'You O.K.?' He knew he hit me so hard, and he was like, 'Hey, are you O.K.?' I said, 'Yeah, no problem.' I never show anyone I'm hurt. Never."

That's the kind of kid Irvin Favre raised. Little more than 24 hours after his dad's death, Favre had one of the greatest games of a career that will surely be followed by a first-ballot election into the Pro Football Hall of Fame. Playing with a broken right thumb that has plagued him since mid-October, he threw for 399 yards and four scores in a 41–7 rout of the Raiders on Dec. 22. He had another efficient day against the Seahawks, completing 26 of 38 attempts for 319 yards and a touchdown, and helping set up Ahman Green for a pair of one-yard, fourth-quarter scoring runs. Then, 4:25 into overtime, cornerback Al Harris capitalized on the only turnover of the game, intercepting a Matt Hasselbeck pass and returning it 52 yards for the winning score.

LAMBEAU FIELD HAS BEEN THE SITE OF COUNTLESS EXCITING games during the Packers' storied history, but not many could match the drama on Sunday. The game was tied at 3, 13, 20 and 27. Seattle rallied from a 13–6 halftime deficit on a pair of one-yard touchdown runs by Shaun Alexander. Green answered with his two scores. Then, with 51 seconds left, Alexander's third touchdown run of the second half, also from a yard out, sent the game into overtime.

For the Seahawks, the loss will sting for months, especially for coach Mike Holmgren, Green Bay's former coach, and Hasselbeck, who gamely matched his mentor, Favre, throw for throw. A 1998 sixth-round draft pick of the Packers who was traded to Seattle in 2001, Hasselbeck completed 25 passes in 45 attempts for 305 yards. He woofed affectionately at his former teammates. And after Seattle won the overtime coin toss, Hasselbeck said over referee Bernie Kukar's field mike for all the world to hear: "We want the ball, and we're gonna score!"

The shame is, Hasselbeck will be remembered mostly for an interception that apparently wasn't his fault. Facing third-and-11 at the Seattle 45-yard line, Hasselbeck sensed a blitz and audibled to a shorter set of routes for his receivers. The Packers sent their Population Blitz—three extra rushers, all coming from the same side—and Hasselbeck threw quickly to wideout Alex Bannister flanked to the left. But Bannister didn't cut his route short. Harris jumped the pattern, picked the ball cleanly and pranced into the end zone. It was the first time in NFL postseason history that an overtime game was won on a touchdown scored by the defense.

Green Bay, riding a five-game winning streak, advanced to a divisional playoff on Sunday against the NFC East champion Eagles in Philadelphia. It was to be the first postseason meeting between the teams since the 1960 NFL title game, the only playoff game that Vince Lombardi ever lost.

On Sunday several WE BELIEVE signs could be seen around Lambeau, held high by fans who think that something more than coach Mike Sherman's strategy is determining the outcome of Green Bay's games. "There are angels watching over us," Packers wide receiver Donald Driver said last week, with a very straight face. "Curly Lambeau, Vince Lombardi . . . and last but not least, Irvin Favre. Don't ask us to explain it, but miracles are happening to us. That's what we believe."

JAMES V. BIEVER/WIREIMAGE.COM

Throughout Brett's life, on and off the field, Big Irv had been a guiding hand.

As the regular season wound down, Green Bay's playoff outlook was grim. On the day before the game against the Raiders, Favre and the rest of his golf foursome—backup quarterback Doug Pederson, kicker Ryan Longwell and punter Josh Bidwell—were hustling to beat the sunset on the 18th hole of a course near the team's Berkeley, Calif., hotel. Pederson got a call from Favre's wife, Deanna (Brett wasn't carrying his cellphone), who told Brett his father had died. Irvin had suffered an apparent heart attack near his home in Kiln, Miss., swerved off the road and died instantly. Brett was famously close to his dad, who was his football and baseball coach during high school, and the question was, Would Brett be too distraught to play against the Raiders?

"Never crossed my mind," Favre said last Friday in his first extended comments about the hours and days after his father's death. "What I do today is a direct result of his influence on my life. When I saw Mike Sherman, he said, 'You want to go home, go.' I said, 'Mike, I'm playing. There's no doubt in my mind that's what he would have wanted.' It's almost like I could hear my dad, 'Boy, don't worry about me. I'm fine.' "

FAVRE HATES GIVING SPEECHES, BUT HE TOLD SHERMAN THAT he wanted to talk to the team at its meeting that night. Favre started crying as he walked to the front of the room, then struggled to make it through the four-minute talk. Even as he recounted the speech last Friday, he got choked up. "I loved my dad," he began that night. "I love football. I love you guys. I grew up playing baseball for my dad, and I grew up playing football for my dad. It's all I know. It's my life. I'm playing in this game because I've invested too much in the game, in you, in this team, not to play. If you ever doubted my commitment to this team, never doubt it again."

"There wasn't a dry eye in the house," Sherman says. "Players, coaches, everybody.

I've never seen a man open his soul so honestly, so completely. It's as clear-cut a picture as anyone's ever seen of this legend."

On the day of the Oakland game, Favre had an unusual feeling. "I've never in my life been scared before a game, but I was scared that night," he says. "Just before the game, Doug Pederson put his hand on my shoulder and said, 'Let's pray,' and I just lost it. Then Mike called everyone up, looked 'em in the eyes and said, 'We're winning this one tonight. We're winning it for Number 4, and we're winning it for Pops.' And I'm thinking, 'Focus. Focus. If you're gonna play, you can't go out and lay an egg.' Everybody would have understood if I had played lousy, but my dad wouldn't have stood for any excuses."

During pregame introductions, the Raiders' crowd was typically merciless, booing as each of the first 10 Green Bay offensive starters ran onto the field. However when Favre's name was announced, the silver-and-black crazies in the Black Hole stood and cheered. "Amazing," Favre says. "I'm hearing this, and I couldn't hardly breathe. It was all I could do to focus on getting out there and playing. It was almost God's way of saying, 'See? There is compassion in this world.' "

Favre completed his first nine passes, for 183 yards and two touchdowns. He threw three bombs as far as he could throw them and hit all three, almost comically amid two and three defenders. "I can't explain it," Favre says. "I'm as amazed as anybody else about what happened." After two quarters he'd thrown for 311 yards—a career-high for a half—and four touchdowns.

Favre's last big cry of the night came on the plane ride back to Green Bay, when he called his mother, Bonita, to see how she was doing. She told him that a couple of weeks before he died Irv had told a friend, "You think Brett's decided who he wants to introduce him when he's inducted into the Hall of Fame? I hope he picks me."

As it turned out the Packers needed the win over the Raiders, plus a victory over the Broncos the next week, plus the Vikings' loss to the woeful Cardinals to get into the playoffs. And with the stubborn Seahawks leading 6–3 midway through the second quarter on Sunday, Green Bay needed something else to go its way. The Packers had a first down at their 20, and Seattle put eight defenders near the line of scrimmage to contain Ahman Green, who has run for 5,685 yards over the past four seasons, the most in football. Favre made a play-action fake to Green, who was swarmed, and threw a strike down the middle to wideout Javon Walker for 44 yards. Four plays later, from the Seattle 23, Favre pump-faked to William Henderson in the right flat, drawing defenders to his fullback, and then turned and threw a laser to tight end Bubba Franks in the end zone.

Favre is 34. He is in his 13th NFL season. He has played in 211 regular season and playoff games. The touchdown pass to Franks was the 377th of his career, yet Favre reacted like it was his first. He spun in the air, pumped both fists, sprinted to the end zone and jumped on Franks, knocking his teammate to the ground with glee.

Yup. This is surely what Irv would have wanted his boy to be doing. ✦

PETER READ MILLER

 MIRACLE MAN If luck is the residue of desire, Favre and the Pack had plenty of both in '03.

Riddell
4

79
4

# LOOK WHO'S BACK ON TOP

BY MICHAEL SILVER

*After another string of misfortunes beset his family and the Packers, Favre again found sanctuary in football*

SI, NOVEMBER 22, 2004

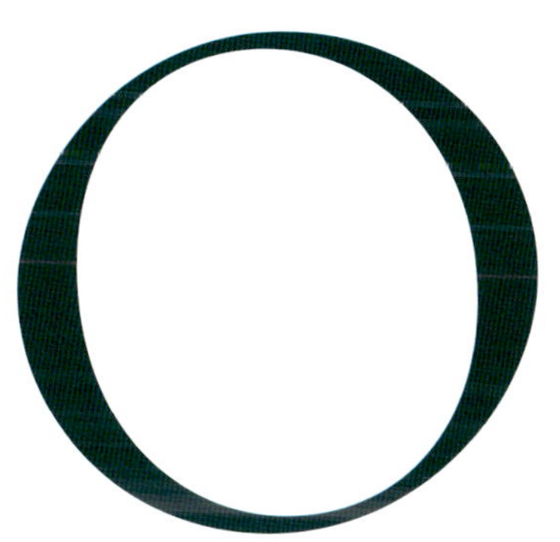

**KAY. SO THE PACK IS BACK, THE LEGEND** lives and all is well in Titletown. That much we know after Brett Favre sent chills through Lambeau Field on Sunday, doing that thing he does so well in leading the Green Bay Packers to a 34–31 last-second victory over the Minnesota Vikings that fully resurrected their championship hopes. Fighting through fear, grief, illness and pain, Favre coped with his problems the best way he knows how, providing 3½ hours of escapist pleasure for a community that devours it like chunks of cheddar. The 35-year-old quarterback's magic touch was never more transcendent than it has been during Green Bay's four-game winning streak over the past month. ✦ Consider how twisted things got after the Pack dropped four consecutive games, including three at Lambeau, to fall to 1–4: Free safety and social butterfly Darren Sharper canceled his annual birthday bash because he was afraid it would look bad, nine offensive linemen drove

JOHN BIEVER

RESCUE HERO With typical flair, Favre turned 2004 from a lost season into a playoff year.

half an hour to devour sushi in the middle of Wisconsin, and coach Mike Sherman's teenage kids waited up for him on several consecutive school nights. "I'd get home around midnight and my son and daughter would be half asleep on the couch," Sherman said last Friday, "just waiting up to make sure that all the sharp utensils were put away."

The coach was kidding, but he wasn't smiling. Even before the leaves change, Green Bay is a cold and forbidding place when the Packers are losing, and when the home team gets humiliated on *Monday Night Football* at Lambeau Field—as the Pack was in a 48–27 loss to the sub-.500 Tennessee Titans in October—the most fervent of Cheeseheads is liable to curse up a bleu streak. "We had no motivation, no enthusiasm, and the fans were letting us hear it," recalled kicker Ryan Longwell, whose 33-yard field goal as time expired provided the winning margin against the Vikings. "They were screaming about Coach Sherman, even yelling things about Number 4, saying it was time to move on."

If the man who wears that jersey, the most famous in franchise history, heard the disparaging words, he wasn't particularly fazed. The graying gunslinger had bigger worries, having lost his brother-in-law, Casey Tynes, in an ATV accident on Favre's property in Mississippi just five days before the Tennessee debacle—and 10 months after the death of Favre's father, Irvin. Three days after the Monday Night Massacre, Favre learned that his wife, Deanna (Tynes's older sister), has breast cancer.

FAVRE FEELS NO NEED TO CAMPAIGN FOR THE SYMPATHY VOTE. "We've received lots of cards, letters, phone calls and flowers, but life goes on, and at some point nobody really cares," Favre said on Sunday night as he sat on a table in the Green Bay training room. "It's a production-oriented business, and if you don't produce, they don't want to hear excuses. I never ask, Why me? because so many great things have happened to me and my family. But, man, when the bad things come, they come in bunches."

Every team experiences its share of heartache, but the Packers have been hit particularly hard. In May 2003 Ray Sherman II, the 14-year-old son of Green Bay's receivers coach, accidentally shot and killed himself. "This is definitely a close-knit team because of all we've been through," says Mike Sherman, who is no relation to Ray. "Adversity can divide you or unite you, and it has united us."

Viewed by some players as detached, a perception that might have something to do with the other half of his dual job, as the Packers' general manager, Mike Sherman opened up to his team in a speech the night before their Oct. 17 road game against the Detroit Lions. Though he has come under fire recently for several personnel decisions—including trading up in the third round of last spring's draft to select a punter (B.J. Sander of Ohio State) who has yet to appear in a regular-season game—Sherman believes he has a roster of players with character, and he spoke about some of their trials. Then Sherman told his players, "Guys, we're in a giant hole, and the only people who can get us out of it are in this room. We're going to have to fight our way out, together."

The Packers routed the Lions 38–10, and they were on their way. Of course, it helps when you play in the NFC, which features two good teams (the Philadelphia Eagles and the Atlanta Falcons) and nine that are either a game above or below .500, including all four in the NFC North: The Packers and the Vikings, losers of three straight, are tied for first place at 5–4; the Lions and the Chicago Bears are 4–5.

There was precedent for the Pack's resurgence: Last year Green Bay sputtered to a 3–4 start before a 30–27 road victory over the Vikings sparked a 7–2 finish. The Pack won the division because the Vikings, who started 6–0, dropped seven of their last 10 games. "If we want to end the perception that the same thing is happening, we have to do something about it," Vikings coach Mike Tice said on the Saturday before the game. "One of the things I plan to tell our team is not to worry if some calls go against us in this game—it's Brett Favre and Lambeau Field, and that's just the way it is."

Give Tice points for clairvoyance, for the game may have hinged on an official's call. After Daunte Culpepper threw a scoring pass to halfback Moe Williams with 1:20 remaining to tie the score at 31, Green Bay's Robert Ferguson busted a long kickoff return up the right sideline but fumbled near midfield after being stripped by Antoine Winfield. Minnesota's Derek Ross appeared to fall on the ball, but after a lengthy pile-up officials ruled that the Packers' Ben Steele—whom the Vikings had cut in training camp (ouch!)—had recovered, setting up Favre's game-winning drive.

When the call went Green Bay's way, at least one visitor from Minnesota was ecstatic—Gunnar Frerotte, the seven-year-old son of Vikings backup quarterback Gus Frerotte. Clad in his prized number 4 Packers jersey, Gunnar declared before the game that even if his father were to start for the Vikings, he would still be rooting for Favre. "Clearly, I've done a hell of a job raising him," joked Gus, who shouldn't feel overly dissed. After all, Favre still skips across the field with a boy's enthusiasm, and with whispers of his possible retirement perpetually in the air (he's noncommittal on the subject) each of his Sundays at play should be appreciated. So should the pranks of this first-ballot Hall of Famer who, last Thursday, left a bagged deer hide in the locker of cornerback Al Harris. "Al didn't know what the hell it was; he threw it halfway across the locker room," says Sharper.

Football, Favre acknowledges, is his sanctuary in times of distress. And so Favre's pain is a Packers fan's gain. Just as he played one of the finest games of his career in a Monday night victory over Oakland last December less than 48 hours after his father's death, Favre has been brilliant since learning of Deanna's illness. Beginning with a 50-yard scoring strike that third-year wideout Javon Walker, an emerging star, snatched away from Minnesota cornerback Brian Williams on the game's eighth play from scrimmage against the Vikings, Favre was in complete command, hitting 20 of

29 attempts for 236 yards, four touchdowns and no interceptions. At times it seemed like 1996 again, with Todd Rundgren's *Bang the Drum All Day* blaring as various players took turns doing the Lambeau Leap.

As in those glory days, the Pack is blessed with a balanced attack. Some of the credit goes to Sherman, who took over play-calling duties when offensive coordinator Tom Rossley underwent an angioplasty before the Detroit game; Green Bay has averaged 35.3 points in the four games since. And some goes to the fabulous linemen who opened holes for Ahman Green and kept Favre from being sacked. The linemen are brave too. "We all have dinner together every Thursday, and we've been going to this sushi place in Appleton ever since we started our streak," says left guard Mike Wahle, one of the league's most underrated players. "It's the only sushi place around, and come to think of it, it isn't very crowded."

Call them Hamachiheads, though it's tough to imagine many Packers fans showing up with raw-fish replica headgear. The 70,671 zanies at Lambeau were treated to one of the season's best matchups, despite the absence of Vikings wideout Randy Moss, who missed the game with a strained hamstring. Favre, who made his 198th consecutive start, was impressed by Culpepper's refusal to throw up his hands and yell, "No Moss!"

"Hey, I'm a huge Randy Moss fan," Favre said, "but Daunte has gotten better with him being out. Now he doesn't just kill you with his arms and his legs; he's killing you with his head too."

In the end, though, Favre, as he so often does, fired the fatal shot. On second-and-10 from the Green Bay 46 with 1:05 remaining, the Packers came out with an empty backfield, got the two-deep zone they were seeking and sent Walker in motion to the left side, where he joined fellow wideouts Ferguson and Donald Driver. The logical target was Driver, who ran a streak down the middle of the field, but when has Favre ever been burdened by percentages? Counting on the element of surprise, he lofted a pass along the right sideline toward backup running back Tony Fisher, who made a leaping catch for a 25-yard gain. Three plays later Longwell drilled the game-winner, and Favre looked to a luxury box behind the Packers' bench and waved to Deanna and their daughters, Brittany and Breleigh.

Brett says doctors expect Deanna, who is scheduled to start chemotherapy later this month, to make a full recovery. Her illness has forced the quarterback to keep his own ailments in perspective—he played on Sunday with a sinus infection, for which he'd been taking antibiotics for several days, and he'd been kept awake for much of the previous night by nasal congestion and neck pain.

"The bottom line is I am old," says Favre, still devoid of pretense after all these years and MVPs. "I'm slower, heavier and more broken down"—he raised and flexed his right arm—"but this . . . . "

Favre didn't finish the sentence, but he didn't have to. The boyish grin said it all. ✦

PAUL SAKUMA/AP



POWER COUPLE Deanna and Brett have stood side-by-side through tough times.

CLARKE HINKLE
1932-41
ROBERT (CAL) HUBBARD
1929-33, 1935
JAMES LOFTON
1978 - 86
FAVRE
4

# HUCK FINN'S LAST RIDE

BY JEFF MACGREGOR

*As questions of retirement hung over Lambeau, the author discovered how deeply the Favre phenomenon still resonated*

SI, DECEMBER 4, 2006

**GO NORTH, TO WHAT SEEMS THE FARTHEST** reach of America, the topmost latitude of the world. It isn't, but it can feel that way, even in the hot dazzle of high summer. Roll past the dairy barns red as bud roses and the storybook milk cows spattered black and white, and the U-Pik strawberry patches and the outlet-store billboards, and the hills swelling soft beneath them all. Drive north to Green Bay. ✦ That this is not the northernmost home of American professional football is merely geographical fact. In our mythology it remains the Fortress of Solitude—frozen in its ancient fame and its lonely arctic greatness—the holiest, most remote outpost in the NFL. Lambeau Field, the city's heart and the first thing you see as you cross the Fox River, looms huge above the bridges and the tree line and the tidy homes strung along the tidy sidewalks. In late July of a new football season the noise of joy and human struggle fills these streets. ✦ Before you've even parked the car, you'll hear and

WALTER IOOSS JR.

HEARING FOOTSTEPS Favre had wavered before deciding to return for the 2006 season.

feel the grunt and thud and the cheering. Packers training camp is under way. This little town, so distant from so many of us that it feels set at the edge of the world—as all small places not our own must—has again become the center of something.

The practice field is just across from the stadium. There are hundreds of people here, families in from Appleton, Eau Claire, Racine and Fish Creek, Manitowoc and Wausau and Waukesha, the mothers and fathers and sons and daughters of Wisconsin standing five deep in the summer funk. On the field is the football team, scores of young men sweating and swearing and thundering back and forth in their iridescent green and gold. One of them stands at midfield, lofting passes with an easy motion and a rhythm like received grace. Each ball cuts a long, sharp arc through the air. "That's it!" yells a woman as the footballs rise and fall. "Way to throw!"

She yells this to the man most of them have come to see, and on whom their season, and their psychic fortunes, will rise or fall. He is slender in the fat shadows of the bellies and bull necks around him, slight and nearly boyish. With his three-quarter-length pants and low-cut socks and his shoes hidden in that deep grass, he appears to be playing barefoot. From the sideline the close-cropped hair still looks blond, and the freckled right arm is still loose and strong, and the smile and the smirk still say, "All right, then, I'll go to hell." Thus, with every attribute in place but the bamboo fishin' pole, here is the NFL quarterback rendered as Huck Finn grown.

To read the dour columnists this year, though, Huckleberry should be taking his first snap under center this season from the comfort and safety of his Medicare-approved personal scooter. Candy-apple red, perhaps, with a handlebar shopping basket, a bicycle bell, and an AARP bumper sticker that reads: I BRAKE FOR GRANDCHILDREN. Because, they say, Brett Favre—Huck Finn grown and now grown old—shouldn't be playing football. Our heroes must never grow old.

And yet here he is.

The Bipolar Romantic Disorder gripping Wisconsin could be described this way: We love Brett. But we love him in inverse proportion to the number of INTs he throws. We love him, but not at the expense of rebuilding the program. We love Brett, but not at the risk of another 4–12 season. We love him, but this is Titletown, U.S.A., after all. Business is business. They'd all be heartbroken if he left them, of course; he's one of the best there ever was. He has brought them a decade and a half of winning, of honor and glory, of mostly wholesome excitement and family thrills and civic pride. A Super Bowl trophy. Three MVP awards. But that 4–12 season in 2005 was heartbreak of a kind too. And, well, sort of embarrassing.

So through the impatient winter and spring, wrestling the notion of retirement, he was cursed by anyone with a microphone or a keyboard for being, like Hamlet, indecisive or half mad; or worse, of feigning indecision or madness in service only of his own selfishness. Still others saw him as Lear, an aging king wandering the wilderness, trying desperately to remember whom and what he really loved; and who and what loved him in return.

TO INTERVIEW BRETT FAVRE IN THE BASEMENT AT LAMBEAU is to sit awhile face-to-face with the phenomenon of American celebrity. There is the private person, of course, and there is the public persona. Often enough these two are utter opposites, even when each can fit the other like a second skin. Favre is, though, as he appears.

In the chair across the table is a young man. Thirty-six, soon to be 37, he is certainly young, except as measured by the accelerated standards of professional sports. By the harsh arithmetic of the NFL, Favre is Methuselah.

Off the field and out of the shadows of those double-wide linemen, he is, at last, large. Tall and broad, he is also gray-haired. He is wearing a forest green T-shirt, baggy gold shorts and flip-flops. On one thick wrist he wears a large dive watch. He sits back in his chair, relaxed but a little wary, alert, summer tan and easy in his body and ready to field questions. Never having seen him before, one might reasonably conclude that Favre was at a job interview for the position of assistant scuba instructor on a cruise ship.

Upstairs, though, in the Lambeau Field Atrium, a cathedral of memory and commerce, the fans wander the shops and restaurants reverent as acolytes, knowing to their bones who and what Brett Favre is. They buy his autobiography and his autograph, his cookbook and his bobblehead with authentic game day stubble. They buy his jersey and his jacket and his pint-sized souvenir helmet. At Brett Favre's Two Minute Grill, they buy his cheeseburgers. And as the video highlights unspool on the monitors hung from the ceiling, they tip their heads back, still chewing, and stare at his great moments on the field as if watching an eclipse. He is already memorialized, enshrined even as he sweats and groans through two-a-days.

Q: There has to be a point for an older player, during the first couple of weeks of camp, when you're shaking the rust off, and your passes are two feet too far or two feet short, that you ask yourself, *Is this the new me, is this the new reality?*

A: Yeah—*Is this the beginning of the end?* I hear that all the time. When you've played 16 years you know that it's just a matter of time before arm strength, or your legs, give out. You're always wondering . . . I come into camp now, my mind's still telling me I can make that throw. But will my body tell me that? My game's always been about throwing from awkward positions and making throws that other people wouldn't make.

He pauses. "And if I can't do that, I can't play."

Whenever Favre jogs onto the practice field with that delicate, slightly pigeon-toed gait, he looks like a man with a stone in his shoe. After starting 241 consecutive NFL games, he is as well-conditioned as he's ever been, but he carries forward all the antique injuries, the catalog of his mortifications: right side, left side, top, bottom, feet, ankles, knees, hands, shoulders, hips, ribs, arms—sprained, sprung, pulled, bruised, broken, separated, cracked, torn, cut, shattered. Annually, if mostly lightly, concussed. By lore and acclamation, the toughest man in the game. Having admitted in 1996 that he was addicted to painkillers, it might take him a while longer to realize that what he may be addicted to is pain.

On Family Night at Lambeau, in August, more than 60,000 fans turn out to sizzle the brats and watch an intrasquad scrimmage. The Packers look good. But then, they're only playing the Packers. Against his teammates, firing left, right and center, long and short, Brett Favre looks like himself. But is he? Against other teams, ominously, he goes 1–3 in the preseason.

FIRST GAME OF THE REGULAR SEASON, HOME AT LAMBEAU against the Bears, and the stadium is ringed with the tailgating faithful. Inside, as part of the pregame ceremony, Reggie White's name is unveiled, to great cheers, on the stadium's upper deck. To lesser cheering, some members of the Packers' 1996 Super Bowl–winning team are then introduced.

Across the field, standing with his arms folded, as if waiting for a bus, is Brett Favre. He played with these guys. But rather than standing with them now in Dockers and sport shirts, 10 or 15 or 50 pounds overweight and looking forward to a Leinenkugel in the stands, he's trying to calculate the likelihood 20 minutes hence of Brian Urlacher's snapping his spine. The Bears are introduced to a chorus of well-mannered Lutheran booing.

Nobody knows yet how good Chicago is, but before the jet exhaust from the F-18 flyover has cleared, the Bears score an easy touchdown on a 49-yard pass. Now they know. The hallmark moment for the Packers comes when Favre's center steps on Favre's foot and flattens him. Things get no better. Final, 26–0 Bears. The Packers' first home shutout in more than 15 years.

At the postgame press conference, rookie Green Bay coach Mike McCarthy is asked if at any point he thought about pulling Favre for young Aaron Rodgers, the backup. "I didn't consider Rodgers," says McCarthy, his face sour, his answer final. Favre isn't even out of the shower yet, and the columnists are agitating for a coup.

Ten minutes later, Favre arrives. His hands on the podium are as raw and red as a fishmonger's. "I was optimistic," he says. "I thought we might surprise a lot of people." He looks to the back of the room, and beyond it. "We can do better than that," he says. But his eyes say he isn't sure.

The next week at Lambeau, the Saints roll in. Again, no one is sure how good they might be. For the game's first 15 minutes they are awful, and the Packers take a 13–0 lead. Thereafter, however, the Packers ease themselves, mistake by mistake, out of the game. Later, in a sullen locker room, Favre says, "We've got to find ways not to lose."

On Internet message boards, posts like this begin to appear: *Jury's in. Favre's out.*

But the truth, as ever, is more complicated. Favre, still mobile, smart and strong, is playing well enough to rank mid-pack among big-name quarterbacks. Surrounded by inexperience and playing behind an offensive line that starts three rookies most weeks, he is, by the hard evidence of the numbers, outplaying press box favorites like Vick, Roethlisberger, McNair, Plummer and Manning the Younger.

Week 3 sends Green Bay to Detroit. Favre arrives at his team's fancy hotel wearing a striped sport shirt, baggy khaki pants and scuffed walking shoes. Had he not stepped off the team bus, hotel management might have thought he'd come to skim the pool.

Over one shoulder he totes a battered canvas bag. In that small olive-drab duffel are hunting magazines and crossword puzzles sufficient to thwart boredom until game time. His pregame meal is already on its way up to his room. Cheeseburger. Fries.

Q: Is it tough being on such a young team?

A: There was a time when I thought, *I'll play forever. This game's easy. What are they worried about? Why study this play if I won't ever run it?* But sure enough, you run it. And so you learn to expect the unexpected. Be ready for any situation. It's never as good as it looks; it's never as bad as it seems. That said, I don't know if we're good enough, right now, to win a lot of games. Some people say, 'Hey, in a couple of years, this team. . . . ' Well, I'll probably be cutting the grass by then.

Q: What about the rumors you'll be traded?

A: There are those who say, 'He shouldn't have come back. Serves him right they're losing. He knew what he was getting into,' and those who say, 'I wish he'd get with a good team and finish out his career right.' And I guess there's a third take too, of those who just don't give a s---. All three, I guess, are fair.

YOU KNOW IT'S GAME DAY IN DETROIT WHEN THE HOMETOWN fans pissing in the alley behind the old JL Stone Company building turn their backs politely to the boulevard. Just up Brush Street at Ford Field, the Packers are trading sucker punches with the Lions. ✦ Learning a new system, a new offense, Favre has new reads and new checkdowns and new routes and new teammates and a new head coach. There are rookies colliding everywhere around him and strange new diagrams from the immense playbook running together in his head and unlined faces of players he hardly knows looking back at him for the ball. There are moments in

JOHN BIEVER

Favre has forever astounded observers with his trademark seat-of-the-pants quarterbacking.

the pocket when it's easy to see his frustration. Seven-step drop, quick, but then his feet stop moving and he stands briefly flat-footed. *Who are these people?* Then a short pump fake, a shake of his head—*This has to be wrong, doesn't it?*—then the throw, almost angry, a recrimination, to a stranger running to the wrong spot at the wrong time. Walking back to the huddle, he's still shaking his head. *Was that him or me?* he wonders.

And moments, too, like this: Favre drops back into a collapsing pocket, chaos everywhere around him, and sets up. Up on the balls of his feet, he stands very still while the noise and the violence grasp at him, then steps forward into a long throw. The ball sails and hangs and lands without a sound in the hands of rookie wide receiver Greg Jennings. He goes 75 yards for a touchdown, and hope gains a few yards on reality. Favre runs the length of the field to gather him up. It is Favre's 400th career TD pass.

Most of the second half looks like a pickup game. Over an afternoon riddled with bad choices and bad bounces, Green Bay clings to a thin victory, 31–24.

"It's just great winning," Favre says outside a locker room smelling of Seabreeze and baby powder, and looks like he means it. "It's a hell of a lot easier to lose a game than it is to win it. We gotta find ways to end these games. But, man, that was fun."

Then Philadelphia. A Monday night game, and down below the press box Eagles fans warm up by shouting pregame obscenities at ESPN's pregame broadcast team. As the sun sets, Philly's trademark vibe of imminent weirdness sets in. The home team comes pouring out through the inflatable Levitra tunnel for its introduction.

For the first half it's mostly Packers. Favre is 15 of 26 for 126 yards. Five minutes into the third quarter, though, the momentum shifts. There is no tipping point, no clear instant in which the worm turns. The Eagles simply score 24 unanswered points and win going away.

With 6:19 to play Favre gets planted hard and hobbles off with a shoulder stinger and a ringing head. "Man, that was a rough one," he says 20 minutes later. "I've got a splitting headache. I just need to get in bed and get some rest."

In another too-quiet clubhouse, this one smelling of wintergreen and wet feet, he leans against a wall. He eats a hot dog. He keeps his back to the room. Questions, sound bites and sentence fragments float past him on the steam from the showers, the damp postgame catechism:

"What happened out there?"

"They just made some plays. . . . "

"Talk about what you do now. . . . "

"This team's gonna do well this year. . . . "

" . . . game like that, you've got to be able to finish. . . . "

" . . . sure I made a mistake or two."

Favre turns, still bleary, to survey the scene. The room, and his thoughts, are slightly out of focus. His bell has been rung, hard, tolling another game played, another battle fought and lost, another step toward the end of things. He sits gingerly on the edge of his locker. He bends but can't reach to tie his shoes. He sits up slowly, waits, then puts his hands to his knees and pushes himself upright. He wobbles there a second. After midnight, laces flapping, he shuffles into the trainer's room.

IN THIS AGE OF CORPORATE QUARTERBACKING, WHEREIN ALL directives come down from the head office, and the position is really no sexier or more autonomous than that of a regional operations manager, Favre remains a "gunslinger." No Green Bay offensive series of more than four or five plays can be broadcast on television without the use of that word. "He's always been a gunslinger," the announcer will say after Favre completes another 27-yard slingshot off his back foot among four converging defenders, or launches a ball into the third row of seats.

An evocative signifier of Old West courage, swagger, improvisation and marksmanship, *gunslinger* also implies a sort of willful and counterproductive recklessness. In an era of quarterbacks praised for their clock-management skills and their low-key willingness to meet the weekly yardage quota nine feet at a time, it's a compliment that takes away as much as it gives.

*Swashbuckler* is another chestnut of the broadcast booth. In fact the nature and number of clichés Favre attracts would make for a potent drinking game. And since he himself has long since sworn off, hoist a few in his honor. Drink a shot of redeye when you hear *gunslinger.* A dram of rum for *swashbuckler.* A glass of wine whenever an announcer uses the phrase *vintage Favre.* Drink a mug of Ovaltine when you hear *He looks like a kid out there.* Chug whenever you hear *He's just trying to make something happen* or *He threw that one off his back foot.* And if you're a Packers fan, drink a double shot and turn off the television when you hear *He tried to force that one in there.*

ST. LOUIS BEATS THE PACKERS THE FOLLOWING SUNDAY. A BAD loss. In the last minute the Green Bay pocket collapses deep in Rams territory, and the ball is batted from Favre's hand. This is variously described by the sporting press as a "backside containment failure" or a "Favre fumble." He walks off the field shaking his head. And so another love note to Favre from the Internet, the endless electronic American id: *Knowing the team is so bad, why bother coming back? Is it ego or stupidity?*

The Packers' bye week at last arrives. Favre visits Hattiesburg, Miss., to watch his eldest daughter, Brittany, a senior at Oak Grove High, play in a regional volleyball tournament. He spends most of the rest of his free time in a tree stand far out in the Wisconsin woods. The leaves fall and the deer come and go beneath him while he sits in solitude.

His wife, Deanna, and his younger daughter, Breleigh, have errands to run, however, and plenty to do. Even in the midst of such a titanic struggle as an NFL season and the losing campaign against time itself, there's school and the grocery shopping and, on a rainy autumn afternoon, gym class.

Deanna Favre, tough, beautiful and practical, waits in the car while Breleigh tumbles and cartwheels. She keeps her hands on the wheel while talking about the decision that led them all back to Green Bay for another year.

Q: How has this fall been for you, watching the Packers play?

A: It's been a little bit difficult, because I've been with Brett for so long, and we're used to winning. Last year and this year have been stressful, seeing how frustrated he is from the lack of wins.

Q: Any second thoughts about his playing this year?

A: I think I've changed my mind as many times as he has. But in his heart he still wanted to play, and still believed he could.

Q: Is he having fun?

A: He has his moments.

Q: Does the criticism of him bother you?

A: I do take it personally. Breleigh's in the second grade; kids come up to her at school and say, 'Your dad stinks! The Packers stink!' She comes home crying. Brittany, the day after the New Orleans game, walked into one of her classes and the teacher—the whole class is sitting there, the bell rings, it's quiet—looks at Brittany and says, 'Must be pretty bad if you let the Saints beat you.' Hello?

The Favres live in a nice house in a nice suburb a few minutes from the stadium. Nothing special. Could be anybody living behind those pale bricks. Banker, lawyer, regional operations manager. And it is somehow heartwarming to see that neighborhood teenagers, in the runup to Halloween, or as a pointed comment on the season to date, have TP'd the tree in the Favres' front yard.

In Week 7 it's a win at Miami, so surprising and joyful that after one touchdown Favre hoists wide receiver Donald Driver over his shoulder. And a week later, a win that surprises no one, at home against the Cardinals. Then a loss to woeful Buffalo, away, followed by a win against the Vikings indoors at the Hump.

DOWN IN THE PACKERS' LOCKER ROOM, AS STYLISH AND contemporary and transient-seeming as the first-class lounge at the Copenhagen airport, and where the Dupont Registry yacht catalogs sit side by side with the backgammon boards and the balls of discarded ankle tapes, they rally each week around Favre. Driver, who has played eight seasons with the Packers, many as the marquee wingman in Favre's flying circus, distills the ideal of teamwork to its earnest essence when asked if he and Favre are, after all the yards and all the years, friends. "No," he says empathically. "We're brothers."

Then it's the Patriots and another bad shutout at home. Favre goes out for the first time this year, with ulnar nerve damage to his throwing elbow. In other words, insult to injury, a hard shot to the funny bone. It was a game no one expected the Packers to win, but still.

So Favre, indestructible, and poised to break almost every career passing record in football, headed into the Monday night game against Seattle with 2,368 passing yards, 13 TDs and seven interceptions. Playing in accord with the tip sheets, Seattle wins.

Now 4–7 with five to play, there are hints and glimmers of the solid team they might one day become. And while their teeter-totter inconsistency is evident and their youthful progress slow, the ambivalence of Green Bay fans to their mythic quarterback hardens and softens from day to day and series to series and play to play. They can't bear to see him go. Nor can they bear to see him falter.

The Packers' record is fittingly ambiguous in a season this crazy, in which none of the experts have been able to predict a thing. The Packers are a little better than anyone gave them credit for being. Only the talking-head handicappers and the Hawaiian-shirt radio talkers seem disappointed that they aren't better. Or worse.

The rest of us, like Brett Favre, try to take our joy in the play. The story of Favre's incomplete pass at retirement this off-season, and the upset, confusion and outrage it caused among so many strangers has, for the most part, come and gone, overtaken by other, more urgent quarterback controversies. But that story will return, told in the same unforgiving way, in the next season or the next or the next. Because the story of Brett Favre's end was never just about him. It is about us.

We need our heroes and household gods forever young, forever strong, forever smart or beautiful. Because we ourselves are not. The end of an elite athlete's career at 25 or 35 or 40 mirrors too perfectly the diminishments and compromises we will see all too well in ourselves at 55 or 65 or 70. The aches and pains and confusion, the missteps, the injury and illness and loss, the memories flown and the flowering of cowardice in the face of uncertainty, all the greatness so far behind you.

Young poets mock the inexorable unwinding of time, until, if they're lucky, they become old poets. Old poets are smart enough to mock only themselves.

Because maybe worse than bad eyes, bad ears, bad back, bad hair, bad heart, is bad faith. Doubt. The delicate stress fracture of the will and the hairline crack along the backbone. *Do I dare to eat a peach?* Mettle fatigue. This is how you calibrate your own descent, in the sad calculus of who you once were, but can never be again.

Which is why the images of Unitas at the end, or Namath, or Ali or Joe Louis, or any of hundreds and hundreds of others, were too much for us. Not because we couldn't muster sufficient sympathy, but because we had altogether too much empathy. To see their sad end warned us too vividly of our own.

And now America is angry at Huck Finn for going gray. And for reminding us, yet again, of our own mortality.

THERE WILL COME A TIME WHEN BRETT FAVRE CAN NO longer play. This is not that time. But at the end of this season—or the next or the next or the next—he will step away at last, having earned the peace of an endless off-season. The cold and the snow will overtake Green Bay, and the stadium at this edge of the world will stand empty behind us, the last thing we see in the rear-view mirror as we cross that river, the light at last failing in the trees.

But until that moment, Brett Favre will be throwing, in a way, for us all. Throwing hope forward, in a single clean step or with a motion as rushed and awkward as man falling out of the tub, as hurried and off-balance as the rest of us. Banking on the past while trying to read a second or two into his future, drilling clean arcs on our behalf into the weakening light and the rising odds, every stand he makes in the pocket another little long shot fired against the infinite and inevitable. Every throw a moment for hope, a defiant line, bright in the air, against chaos and diminishment and the final goodbye. ✦

WALTER IOOSS JR.

 BRIGHT OUTLOOK Toward the end of '06, Number 4 showed his right arm had plenty left.

Riddell
NFL

86

# TOP OF THE CHARTS

BY PETER KING

*It was another classic Favre moment as he surpassed Dan Marino to become the alltime NFL leader in touchdown passes*

SI, OCTOBER 8, 2007

**HAT BETTER WAY FOR ONE OF THE** biggest records in America's favorite game to fall than for Brett Favre to improvise a play at the line and execute it with the flair that has made him America's favorite quarterback? It helped to see the action unfold live on on Sept. 30 in Minneapolis, because the clip that would air later that day on the highlight shows did not do justice to Favre's 421st career touchdown pass, the one that moved him past Dan Marino atop the alltime list. The replay had Favre lasering a 16-yard touchdown pass to wideout Greg Jennings, the first points in a 23–16 Packers win over the Vikings that lifted Green Bay to 4–0. But that brief clip started eight seconds late and didn't reveal the full story of the play—nor why it exemplified Favre's unflagging mastery of his position. ✦ So let's start with eight seconds left on the play clock, the Packers with third-and-seven at the Minnesota 16-yard line late in the first quarter, and the noise in

JOHN BIEVER

BIG SHOULDERS Jennings got a happy ride into history after catching Favre's 421st.

the Metrodome sounding like the takeoff runway at O'Hare on a Friday at 5 p.m.
**:08** . . . As Favre, in the shotgun, prepared to take the snap from center Scott Wells, he looked up and saw two reasons to worry: To Favre's left, linebacker E.J. Henderson was fixing to blitz; and to the quarterback's right, about 10 yards up the field, free safety Dwight Smith was positioned directly in the line of Jennings's pass route. Favre realized he had to call an audible. But that noise . . . .

"Today was as loud as I've heard a stadium in recent memory," Favre said afterward. "I think we went on silent snap count on all but two plays [all game]." The audible was Y Dragon: Instead of tight end Donald Lee's running 12 yards upfield, which would encourage Smith to clog the middle, Favre wanted Lee to run a shallow flat route toward the sideline. This would give Jennings, who was split right, single coverage on a quick slant to the post. And the defender covering Jennings would be a rookie nickelback, Marcus McCauley. "I needed a quick-strike play because we probably weren't going to be able to block all they were bringing," Favre said. "Y Dragon was perfect."
**:07 . . . :06 . . . :05** . . . As Favre tried to get his teammates' attention and made the hand signal for Y Dragon, he realized that Lee, tight to the formation next to the right tackle, wasn't acknowledging the audible. So Favre scurried over, slapped the tight end on the butt and signaled the play. "He sees everything," Lee would later say of Favre, "so every decision he makes we know is the right one." Jennings felt a thrill of anticipation: "I'm thinking touchdown."
**:04 . . . :03 . . . :02** . . . Favre dropped back into the shotgun and, still unsure whether the play would come off, thought for a millisecond about calling a timeout. "But if I do," he said, "not only would we probably have changed our personnel group, [but the Vikings] would have changed to match up with us." Favre's eyes darted left to see Henderson edge closer to the line, to a gap that Favre knew he would quickly get through. "I looked up at the clock," Favre said, "but by then I knew it'd be a big play if we could get it off on time." He stomped his foot, signaling Wells to snap the ball.
**:01** . . . At the snap Henderson barreled in from Favre's left. "I knew I only had a second or two," the quarterback recalled. Lee, as directed, darted to the right flat, taking Smith with him and opening the hole in the coverage that Favre needed. Jennings sprinted four yards upfield and pivoted toward the post. "As I got into the route," Jennings said, "I realized how perfect the play was. There was nobody there."

Moments after the play clock hit :00, Favre, as he'd done so often in his career, threw a tight spiral that led his receiver perfectly. The ball hit Jennings between the 8 and the 5 on his white Packers jersey. McCauley trailed him helplessly. "I think I got hit on the play," Favre said. "But I didn't feel anything." Henderson did pop Favre a split second after the pass was released, bouncing the quarterback to the turf.

"I was happy," Favre said. "We got the play off, everybody did what they were supposed to do, there were no flags, and I just thought to myself, This is what an efficient offense is supposed to be—it's supposed to make the plays that are there. Then it took me a few seconds to realize that was the record."

Favre ran to Jennings and lifted him onto his shoulders. He missed Marino's taped tribute on the video screen as he hugged his teammates and handed the ball to Pro Football Hall of Fame vice president Joe Horrigan. Then he embraced his wife, Deanna, who was in the front row, and his thoughts moved past the record. "We've got to win this game now," he said to Deanna. As the Packers kicked off, Favre sat on the bench, flipping through a binder of Polaroids showing Minnesota's defensive formations during the game's first 10 minutes.

IT'S ALL SO UNEXPECTED—GREEN BAY UNDEFEATED AND LEADING the NFC North, the team's eight-game winning streak dating to the previous December, and Favre, who'll be 38 on Oct. 10, turning back the clock in his 17th NFL season. Or is it? Perhaps we shouldn't be surprised, given how he rededicated himself to the job after announcing last February that he was not ready to retire. For four months at home in Mississippi during the off-season Favre had a live-in personal trainer, and he arrived at camp as flexible and fit as he'd been at any point in his career. Because Favre, who stopped drinking in 1999, lives a workaday life in Green Bay during the season—"He just doesn't go out, at all, anymore," Deanna says—the game occupies more of his time than ever.

Each Monday he has the Packers' video staff load his laptop with the previous four games of the upcoming opponent. On Tuesday, the players' day off, Favre goes to the offices at Lambeau Field for four hours, to get a head start on the game plan—and to plant a few seeds in coach Mike McCarthy's head. "He'll give me all kinds of ideas and plays, and I'll have to say no, no, no," says McCarthy. "But there's a few every week I really like. I don't want to speak for him, but I think he sees the light at the end of the tunnel. He wants to make sure he leaves nothing to chance. In the last few weeks, all anyone's talked about is the record. Not with him. The big thing with him is January football. You look in his eyes, and you can see the wars he's been through, trying to get to more January football. It's all he cares about."

Favre remains a compelling figure to anyone who loves the game. "He's still our Michael Jordan," Chiefs quarterback Damon Huard said on Sunday night. "When your game is over on Sunday, you hope you can go home and catch the end of the Packers game, so you can watch Brett."

For now, he's the feel-good story of the 2007 season. He knows it. As Favre walked off the field on Sunday, wading through the photographers and minicams and hangers-on, he looked up and waved to the fans, an unabashedly adoring crowd in a stadium that has not been friendly to him over the years. Then, struggling to be heard over the din, he said, "I guess I can still do it." So we see. ✦

# SPORTSMAN OF THE YEAR

BY ALAN SHIPNUCK

*In a season in which he remade his game at 38 while continuing to inspire on and off the field, Favre earned SI's highest honor*

SI, DECEMBER 10, 2007

**THERE IS NO HAPPIER PLACE THAN GREEN BAY,** Wis., on a Sunday evening after the Packers have won. The beer tastes better, the girls are even prettier, and few seem to notice the bite in the air. In a town defined by its team, civic temperament can be quantified on a scoreboard. In mid-November, moments after the Packers had defeated the Carolina Panthers 31–17 at Lambeau Field, the parking lot was alive with merriment. Kids in number 4 jerseys and GOT BRETT? sweatshirts chased footballs with reckless abandon, tailgaters handed out bratwurst right off the grill, and one optimistic gent tried to sweet-talk the more attractive passersby into adding to the impressive collection of donated bras he had strung up on a flagpole. ✦ The epicenter of Green Bay's game-day good cheer is adjacent to Lambeau, just across Holmgren Way, a block over from Lombardi Avenue: Brett Favre's Steakhouse, located at 1004 Brett Favre Pass. The restaurant ("Where you are the MVP!") is a 20,000-square-foot

WALTER IOOSS JR.

VINTAGE FORM A wiser, more introspective Favre made the Pack a surprise success in 2007.

temple to the Packers quarterback, and following the Panthers game Favre's extended family had gathered in a private back room for a celebration of its own.

Brett's wife, Deanna, was there, looking glamorous in a long coat and high-heeled boots. Even before her memoir about beating breast cancer hit *The New York Times*'s best-seller list, she was the second-biggest celebrity in Green Bay. Favre's mother, Bonita, was holding court at one of the half-dozen tables, her throaty laugh audible over the din. Brett's sister, Brandi, was cooing over her newborn daughter, Myah, while his brothers, Scott and Jeff, were busy refereeing their young sons, who were creating a ruckus by playing tackle football with an empty water bottle. Also enjoying the spread of steak and crawfish and all the fixings were various cousins, neighbors and hangers-on. In this loud, lively gathering only one person was missing—the man for whom the restaurant and the street are named.

In his 16th winter in Green Bay, Favre has turned into Gatsby, throwing a party he no longer enjoys. While his family and friends were reliving every detail of his three-touchdown performance against Carolina, Favre was at home a couple of miles away, stretched out on his couch, watching that day's NFL highlights and cuddling with his lapdog, Charlie. By the ostentatious standards of modern-day celebrity, Favre's house is modest, but it suits him fine. On this Sunday evening it was dark and quiet, giving him some precious hours to decompress. There was a time when Favre never skipped a chance to celebrate—"Hell, I always had to be the life of the party," he says—but now solitude is what he thirsts for.

"As I've gotten older, I've become more of a loner," Favre says. "You've just been out there in front of 80,000 screaming people, everyone watching every move you make, the pressure of all that—it's fine and dandy for three hours, but afterward. . . . " Here Favre takes a big, billowing breath. "I used to thrive on that adrenaline. I never wanted it to end. Now I need to get back to reality. Like sitting on the couch with Charlie."

If Favre is weary, it's only because he has given so much of himself to Green Bay through the years. "He means everything to these people," says Donald Driver, who's in his ninth season catching Favre's passes. "He's not only our leader—he's the symbol of the franchise, of the whole town. There's a generation of fans in Green Bay who don't know this team ever existed without Brett."

When Favre decided to return for the 2007 season, even die-hard Cheeseheads must have been hoping only that he would not tarnish his legacy. What no one expected was that Favre would reinvent himself yet again, enjoying one of his best years at age 38 while cajoling a talented but callow team toward a division title. Along the way he passed several more significant milestones for quarterbacks, overtaking Dan Marino atop the alltime list in touchdown passes, and John Elway in victories by a starter.

But one record above all others speaks to what Favre is made of: his Ripkenesque streak of consecutive starts at quarterback, more than five seasons ahead of the next player on the list, Peyton Manning. During a 37–27 loss at Dallas in Week 13, Favre was knocked out of the game in the second quarter, when on the same play he separated his left shoulder and took a helmet to his right elbow, causing numbness in two fingers on his throwing hand. Afterward, to no one's surprise, Favre said he expected he would not miss a game. He has rarely been flawless (after all, he leads the NFL in lifetime interceptions), but he's always shown up. Through pills and booze, through cancer and car crashes and heart attacks, he has played on. Once reckless on and off the field, Favre has matured before our eyes while never losing his boyish love for the game.

It is for his perseverance and his passion that SI honors Favre with the 54th Sportsman of the Year award. But there is more to his story than on-field heroics. On game day the whole of Green Bay may live and die on Favre's rocket right arm, but his greatest legacy lies in how many people he has touched between Sundays.

THE INTENSITY OF FAVRE'S RELATIONSHIP WITH THE PACKERS faithful goes far beyond mere longevity. He arrived in Green Bay in 1992 through a trade with the Atlanta Falcons, and in the third game of the season came off the bench to lead a madcap comeback against the Cincinnati Bengals, throwing the winning touchdown with 13 seconds left. He has refused to leave the starting lineup ever since, harnessing his hair-on-fire style to win an unprecedented three MVP awards (1995, '96, '97) and lead Green Bay to a Super Bowl triumph following the 1996 season.

But the success was leavened by personal setbacks and heartache. In 1996 the NFL sent him to rehab to kick an addiction to the painkiller Vicodin. Two months later Scott was involved in a car crash that killed his passenger, Mark Haverty, Brett's close childhood friend. Scott pleaded guilty to felony DUI and served a year of house arrest. Brett's own heavy drinking drove Deanna to consult divorce lawyers before Favre checked himself into rehab in '99.

After Favre quit drinking, he settled into the comfortable second act of his career, during which life was quieter and his teams were good but not quite good enough. The drama, however, was far from over. In December 2003 Favre lost his father, Irvin, who suffered a heart attack at age 58. The day after Big Irv died, Favre summoned the defining performance of his career, passing for 399 yards and four touchdowns against the Oakland Raiders and riveting a *Monday Night Football* audience. Grown men around Green Bay still tear up when recalling that game.

One dark week in 2004 set the Favres reeling all over again. In October, Deanna's younger brother, Casey Tynes, was killed when he crashed his all-terrain vehicle, leaving behind a girlfriend who was eight months pregnant. Four days after Casey's funeral, Deanna learned she had breast cancer. As always, the Favres were overwhelmed by the outpouring in Green Bay—bags of letters, innumerable prayer circles and many kind wishes murmured in the grocery aisle.

"People here treat us like family, and I think they care for us like family," says Deanna. "Because of everything we've been through, they don't see Brett as untouchable or as some kind of superhero. And they've been through it with us. The fans here feel close to Brett because they've all had their own similar struggles. Nothing against Tom Brady or Peyton Manning, but I'm not sure their fans relate to them in the same way."

FAVRE GREW UP IN TINY KILN, MISS., "THE KILL" AS IT'S known on the Gulf Coast, a place his coach at Southern Mississippi, Curley Hallman, would memorably describe as "like *The Dukes of Hazzard*, minus the demolition derby." In a typical anecdote from Favre's youth, he was tossing a football to Scott but led him too much, sending his brother through a bay window of the family house. When the Favre boys weren't shooting each other with BB guns or feeding Oreos to alligators from the back porch or sneaking pinches of chewing tobacco—of baby brother Jeff, Favre once said, "That son of a bitch could chew and spit when he was three years old"—they were tagging along to sporting events with their father, who coached high school football and American Legion baseball in Kiln. Under Big Irv's watchful eye, Brett developed into a standout athlete, but he was imbued with none of the aloofness that the star quarterback has in every teen movie.

Credit Bonita for that. During her 16 years as a special-education teacher, Brett was a regular visitor to her classroom—and not just during the two years when Deanna was an aide and he wanted to flirt. (She and Brett met in catechism when they were seven; they began dating when she was a high school sophomore and he was a freshman.)

Of her students, whose conditions ranged from common learning disabilities to severe developmental problems, Bonita says, "There was a time when people like that were locked away, but they have value. They can be productive members of society. I always made it clear to my children they weren't any better than the kids I taught."

Around Kiln there was a developmentally disabled man named Ronnie Hebert, who served as an equipment manager on Brett's youth baseball team and helped out with Big Irv's squads. Sensing that the other players felt awkward about sitting next to Hebert on the bus or sharing a table at restaurants, Brett always made an effort to include him. The two forged a lasting friendship and remained close enough that a few years ago, Deanna surprised her husband by flying Hebert in to be the guest speaker at a fund-raising dinner for Favre's charitable foundation. Says Deanna, "That night is as emotional as I've ever seen Brett, aside from when his dad passed away."

RICH GABRIELSON/ICON SMI

Deanna was on hand in Minnesota when Brett broke Marino's TD mark.

Though Favre has never had difficulty connecting with people, he admits that early in his career he was too busy having a good time to reach out to others. Deanna had become pregnant when she was 19 and did much of the early parenting of daughter Brittany so that Brett could concentrate on football. Deanna and Brittany continued to live in Mississippi during Favre's first few seasons in Atlanta and Green Bay, leaving him unchaperoned. "It was out of control for a while," says Scott. "We'd go into a bar and just take over the place. Brett would be on top of the bar, pouring drinks. The people loved it, of course."

Favre's Vicodin addiction led to a 46-day stay at the Menninger Clinic in Topeka, Kans. "I was able to see some things a little more clearly," Favre says of his time there. "I realized I had become sidetracked in a lot of important ways." In July 1996, shortly after he completed rehab, Brett and Deanna were married. That year he also started the Brett Favre Fourward Foundation, with a charter to provide aide to disabled and disadvantaged children in Mississippi and Wisconsin.

Over the last decade the foundation has given out $4 million to dozens of charitable organizations, focusing its efforts on the kind of kids who remind Favre of Ronnie Hebert. One recent beneficiary was the Miracle League of Green Bay, to which Favre donated $100,000 to help build a baseball facility with a specialized wheelchair-friendly artificial surface. In addition to the field, Favre's money went toward a high end public address system and the retrofitting of the playground equipment to make it more accessible to those with disabilities. "These kids always had to sit and watch before," says Bruce Willems, whose 16-year-old daughter, Kyla, is a regular in the Miracle League. "Now they get to play, and you can't believe what it does for their self-esteem."

In fact, some of the kids have developed big league attitude. Eleven-year-old Jacob Van Den Berg "won't go to bat until his name is announced on the P.A. system," says his father, Jeff. "The fact that Brett Favre helped build this place, that's a big deal to him."

Kids like Kyla and Jacob are kindred spirits with the children of Kiln's Gaits to Success, which provides therapeutic horseback riding for the disabled. With a stable of horses and 10 lush acres, it is not an inexpensive operation, and Carolyn Rhodes, the program's director, says simply, "Without Brett, we would not exist."

The link between Kiln and Green Bay became more explicit after Hurricane Katrina ravaged the Mississippi coast in 2005. Bonita's house was flooded by the storm surge and had to be rebuilt from the ground up. (Since 1997, Brett and Deanna have spent their off-seasons in Hattiesburg, Miss., 70 miles inland, and their house was unaffected.) In the aftermath of the storm, Favre used a couple of Packers press conferences to appeal for help for his home state. An account was set up in Green Bay for contributions, and within eight weeks upwards of a million dollars had poured in. Says Mike Daniels, president of Nicolet Bank, which administered the account, "We had packages arriving full of change, with letters in crayon that said, 'Dear Mr. Favre, this is from my piggybank. Your friends need it more than I do.' "

The Door County Gulf Coast Relief Fund was also born in the wake of Katrina, though its roots could be traced to Super Bowl XXXI, when the Packers beat the New England Patriots at the Superdome in New Orleans, about an hour's drive from Kiln. During the week of the game, many of the Green Bay faithful made the pilgrimage to Favre's boyhood home, and the Broke Spoke, Kiln's main bar, became a sort of downmarket Graceland. It was there that Pete D'Amico of Green Bay first met Big Irv, and a long-standing kinship with Kiln was born. Three days after Katrina struck land, D'Amico and his friend Tony Anheuser were in a borrowed truck, making the 22-hour drive to Mississippi, packing donated clothes, food, water and a couple of hundred steaks, which they cooked up every night in front of the Broke Spoke and handed out to whoever was hungry.

Since then, the relief efforts have continued to grow in scope; Green Bay volunteers—electricians, roofers and other skilled tradesmen in strong demand on the Gulf Coast—have made more than 20 trips to Kiln to help rebuild damaged homes. In October, during the Packers' bye week, 26 Cheeseheads traveled to Kiln. "My whole life has become about giving back the blessings I've been given," says the 66-year-old Anheuser, a retired home-furnishings retailer. "It's through Brett and the connection we have to Kiln that I've found my purpose."

WHEN FAVRE HEARS THESE STORIES, HE CAN ONLY SHAKE his head. "It's pretty hard to fathom," he says of his impact. But he does much more than just raise money and inspire others from afar. At a fund-raiser for Green Bay's Brian LaViolette Scholarship Foundation, Favre came on stage to play drums with the house band. "When that happened, a bunch of us old ladies in the crowd started screaming," says Sue LeTourneau, who helps run the scholarship program named for her nephew, who died in a swimming accident.

JOHN BIEVER

 LONG REACH Favre said he was humbled by his impact on fans from Green Bay to the Gulf.

Riddell
1957-2007
LAMBEAU FIELD

Many athletes give time to the Make-A-Wish Foundation; for Favre it's a regular part of his workweek. So strong is the demand to meet the Packers' quarterback among Make-A-Wish kids with life-threatening medical conditions that Favre schedules a visit nearly every Friday when the Packers are not playing an away game. "It's an honor to be asked," he says, "but I'm not going to lie—it's hard. There are times when it takes a lot out of me. These kids are so cool, but you can't ignore what they're up against and what their families are going through."

In September 2004 Favre met with a six-year-old from Neenah, Wis., named Anna Walentowski. She was suffering from Alexander disease, an extremely rare form of the degenerative brain disorder called leukodystrophy, for which there is no known cure. By the time her visit was arranged, Anna was on a feeding tube for 20 hours a day. In the preceding months she had repeatedly been rushed to the hospital with spasms of her upper respiratory system, which made breathing nearly impossible. "It was a dark, dark time in our lives," says Anna's father, Jeff. "Our little girl was deteriorating pretty rapidly."

Anna's parents feared she would not be strong enough to make the trip to the Packers' practice facility, but she rallied for the big day. Favre had recently been banged up, and the first thing the little pixie in a Packers cheerleading outfit said to him was, "How's your thumb?" The two bonded instantly. Anna's mother, Jennifer, remembers Favre giving her daughter hug after hug and gently helping Anna get in and out of her stroller, so the two could play catch with a Nerf football and later eat lunch with the team.

Before saying goodbye, Anna gave Favre a prayer card with her picture on it. Unbeknownst to the Walentowskis, Favre taped it to his refrigerator door that night, and it stayed there for the rest of the season. "Every day we looked at that picture and prayed for Anna and her family," Deanna wrote in her book, *Don't Bet Against Me!*

In the years since Anna's visit her condition improved dramatically. This is no doubt due to specialized care made possible by the evolving understanding of leukodystrophy. Anna's parents think the meeting with Favre also has had something to do with it. "That one day they spent together never really ended," says Jennifer. "We would often talk about the visit and look at the photos, and she would be asked all the time to tell the story. It became a big part of her life."

The tale took another turn when Deanna's book was published in September 2007, including the passage about Anna, a girl she knew only from the photo on the fridge and the effect she'd had on her husband. The Walentowskis were unaware of their cameo in the book until a friend called to tell them about it—and to say that Deanna was in nearby Appleton at that moment for a book signing. The family hustled over to meet Deanna. Now nine, Anna still faces serious medical challenges, but against all odds she has continued to get better. "She looked so good, so happy," says Deanna. "I couldn't wait to go home and tell Brett. We had often wondered about Anna, about how she was doing. When I told Brett, it touched him. He didn't really have any words. He was pretty choked up."

FUNNY THING ABOUT THE FAVRES IS THAT BRETT ISN'T EVEN THE hottest quarterback in the family. Dylan Favre is a high school phenom for the St. Stanislaus Rockachaws in Bay St. Louis, Miss., having just completed a sophomore season in which he threw 36 touchdown passes, a record for the southern Mississippi section. Brett has taken to mentoring his nephew, but they rarely discuss X's and O's. "That's probably for the better," says Dylan. "If I tried some of the things Uncle Brett does on the field, my coach would kill me!"

So what do they talk about?

"Leadership."

Pressed to define what that means, Uncle Brett says, "It's somehow getting 52 other guys to raise their level of play. To get them to believe in what we're trying to do. You do that by setting an example, by doing things the right way. I've always shown up, I've always been prepared, I practice every day. I practice hard. I study. No matter what happens on the field, I never point blame at anybody else. Everything I do comes back to leadership, the example I want to set."

Favre says he has not given a locker-room pep talk since the eve of the 2005 season. "And we went 4–12 that year," he adds with a chuckle, "so what does that tell you?"

Nonetheless, in 2007 Favre has, by necessity, become more direct in his leadership. Green Bay is the youngest team in the league and especially green on offense; starting running back Ryan Grant is playing his first NFL season, and among the top six receivers only two have been in the league more than two full years. "[Brett's] become a lot more vocal, a lot more hands-on," says Favre's backup, Aaron Rodgers. "He's out there coaching the entire offense, from running back to wide receiver to tight end. In practice he'll break away from what [the quarterbacks] are doing to watch some of the other positions go through their reps. He's extremely engaged in everything that's happening."

The evolution began with a challenge from second-year coach Mike McCarthy, who in the preseason told the future Hall of Famer that he flat-out had to play better. In 2006 Favre threw just 18 touchdown passes, his fewest since his first year with the Packers, and his 56% completion rate was the worst of his career. Favre has always been as much a point guard as a quarterback, forever finding creative (if chancy) ways to deliver the ball. McCarthy's orders for this year were to make safer decisions and substantially improve his completion percentage. "I wish I could

JOHN BIEVER

Rodgers (12) and other young Packers lauded Favre's more active leadership.

make the story better by telling you there was a big knockdown, drag-out fight, but Brett's a pro's pro," says McCarthy. "From Day One he has embraced what we're trying to accomplish."

While Favre can still revert to his free-wheeling ways, he has torn through the league with the most controlled, efficient play of his career. Grant has begun to assert himself, but with the Packers' ground game still coalescing, Favre is completing a career-best 67.4% of his attempts and has thrown only 10 interceptions. On Thanksgiving Day he carved up the Detroit Lions with 20 straight completions, two short of the NFL record, and he has already tied his Packers mark with seven 300-yard games. "He is playing as well as I've seen him play," says Lions coach Rod Marinelli, "and I've [coached] against him since 1996."

With a game-breaking passing attack backed up by an athletic, aggressive defense, the Packers look capable of a deep playoff run. It is a measure of how far this unproven team has come that after the Week 13 loss in Dallas, no one was claiming a moral victory for having played the Cowboys close into the fourth quarter, even with Favre out and injuries sidelining top cornerback Charles Woodson and sack specialist Kabeer Gbaja-Biamila. "Winning is the only thing that matters here, and that comes from Number 4," says rookie receiver James Jones. "A team takes on the mentality of its leader. And this guy is the ultimate warrior. That can't help but filter down."

Favre's influence is felt in many other ways. His improvisational skills belie an obsessive preparation that forces his teammates to keep up. Following the Panthers game, after Favre had relaxed at home with his dog for a while, he sneaked back to a darkened Lambeau to watch game film for an hour and a half. Not that his dedication to his craft prevents Favre from cutting up. "You play your best football when you're loose and relaxed and having a good time," he says. Favre has tried to impart that notion to his teammates, though some of his methods would probably not impress Vince Lombardi. He's notorious for surreptitiously squirting heating ointment into colleagues' jockstraps, and his locker room flatulence is legendary—though if you can believe Green Bay insiders, it is delivered with a purpose. "There have been many times before a game when you can see the guys are kind of tight," says Edgar Bennett, Green Bay's running backs coach and formerly Favre's teammate for five seasons. "Brett always knows how to loosen them up. I don't want to go into too many details, but let's just say that the guy has some unique talents."

WHILE FAVRE SIMULTANEOUSLY INSPIRES AND RELAXES his teammates, he also forms a palpable brotherhood with them. No Packer has felt this more profoundly than receiver Koren Robinson, who has become Favre's personal reclamation project. A first-round pick of the Seahawks in 2001, Robinson has struggled with alcohol abuse for several years. As a Minnesota Viking in 2005 he was voted to the Pro Bowl as a kick returner, but in August 2006 the team cut ties with him after his second arrest for drunken driving. Green Bay took a chance and signed Robinson the next month, but four games into the 2006 season he was suspended by the NFL for a year because of a third violation of the league's substance-abuse policy, the fallout from one of his incidents in Minnesota. Robinson was banned not only from games but also from practicing with the Packers and using any team facilities. When the suspension was handed down, Favre blasted the NFL, accusing the league of turning its back on a player who he thought could clearly benefit from structure and support.

In the year that Robinson was out of football, Favre took it upon himself to provide that safety net, regularly calling Robinson to check up and lend an ear. "For a guy of his stature to reach out, he didn't have to do that," says Robinson, 27. "To know he cared so much for me, it was a huge motivation for me to better myself and correct the things in my life that needed to get right."

Favre's compassion was born of his own experiences. "From a substance-abuse standpoint I was probably worse off than Koren," he says. "People don't realize that, because I was never suspended. But I've done all kinds of drugs, I've drunk too much—the only difference between me and Koren is that I didn't get caught. But I've been there, and I know how lonely it can be."

Robinson, who is married to his college sweetheart, Joy, and is the father of an 18-month-old son, K.J., was reinstated in October of this year, and quickly made an impact on the field. His 67-yard kickoff return against the Panthers was the longest of the season by a Packer, and Robinson was featured in the new five-receiver set Green Bay unveiled in November. Against Detroit, Robinson gave Packers fans a glimpse of his playmaking ability, gaining 50 yards on only two catches. He has scraped off the rust with another assist from Favre. Says McCarthy, "I think sometimes Brett looks to Koren a little too much during practice, just trying to get him involved, get his confidence up."

An NFL locker room is among the most macho places in sports, but Robinson's voice catches when he talks about his quarterback. "I am so blessed to have a friend like Brett Favre," he says. "A lot of what keeps me going now is that I want him to be proud of me."

"I'm already proud of him," says Favre. "I couldn't care less if he ever catches another pass. The way he has put his life back together is much bigger than that."

On the vast expanse of Robinson's right biceps is tattooed MATTHEW 28:20. That scripture appropriately captures Favre's relationship with Robinson and the rest of his teammates: "[Teach] them to obey everything I have commanded you. And surely I am with you always, to the very end of the age."

THE FAVRE HOUSEHOLD IS ABOUT AS CASUAL AS THEY COME, BUT there is one immutable rule. "We don't talk about retirement," says Deanna. "Ever. This whole town is obsessed about what Brett is going to do, so at home it's off-limits because he needs to get away from it."

There is no doubt that Favre has plenty left physically to keep playing, a point driven home during the Panthers game, when he was six years younger than the other starting quarterback, Vinny Testaverde. Ask Donald Driver if Favre has lost anything off his fastball, and Driver says with a laugh, "My fingers can answer that. There's times after practice they tingle a little bit. Guy hasn't lost a thing, except maybe a little hair."

At this point in his career Favre is used to the aches and pains. "Mentally, it's much more demanding," he says. "Now I dwell on the negative a lot more. I'm thrilled to death we're winning, but with each game I feel more pressure to play better, to keep it going. Next play's got to be better, next game's got to be better. The better you play, the higher the expectations become, not only of yourself, but what others expect. It can flat wear you out."

Even as Favre has brought so much joy to Green Bay this year, he has been in the familiar position of playing with a heavy heart. The Favres suffered another personal loss this summer when Deanna's stepfather, Rocky Byrd, died of a heart attack at age 56 while the Packers were in training camp. Rocky had helped to fill the void left by Big Irv's death. This year, for the first time in his career, Favre did not return to Mississippi during the Packers' bye week, choosing to stay alone in Green Bay. "It would have been his first time home since Rocky passed away," says Deanna, "and I don't think he wanted to face that."

Family matters were in the backdrop as Favre considered retirement in the past two off-seasons. In recent years he and Deanna have been separated from older daughter Brittany during the football season. From first through eighth grade she attended school in Green Bay in the fall, then finished the school year in Hattiesburg. Upon reaching high school, however, Brittany insisted she be allowed to stay in Mississippi year-round. She lived with Deanna's sister's family, seeing her father in the fall mostly when she traveled to Green Bay for Packers home games. Brittany is now in college, but eight-year-old Breleigh is following the old routine, splitting time between schools in different states. "It hasn't been easy on the girls," Favre says, "which is not something the public ever factors in."

Favre also longs to spend more time at his 465-acre spread in Hattiesburg, where in the off-season he works the land, including his dozen deer plots. Then there are the two thriving charitable organizations to look after, his Fourward Foundation and the Deanna Favre Hope Foundation. The latter was founded in 2005 to raise breast-cancer awareness and provide assistance for those battling the disease. Deanna has since become a sought-after public speaker, commanding as much as $45,000 for a corporate engagement, all of the money going to the foundation. The pink Packers hats ubiquitous in Green Bay are another revenue stream. The foundation annually gives out dozens of grants for uninsured or underinsured women battling breast cancer.

As the Favres prepare for life after football, the people of Green Bay are also girding themselves for the inevitable. There is a funny feeling in the air around Lambeau this year: Every unexpected win is accompanied by a collective dread that it has inched Favre closer to retirement. Deanna doesn't exactly refute the notion. "He needed to go out like this," she says. "He deserved a year like this. I'm not saying he will or won't [retire after the season], and I don't know what I'd say if he asked me, but he's the kind of competitor who has to go out a winner. That's who he is."

Favre refuses to look beyond each week's game, but he does say, "Sure, I would love to go out with a trip to the Super Bowl, but it doesn't have to end that way. Had I left last year, or even the year before, it's been a great career. I'm content with it." Favre suddenly grows animated, leaning forward in his chair. "I don't know how it's going to end, but I do know this: Throwing a touchdown pass for the Green Bay Packers is pretty neat. I've thrown a ton, and every one of them was a helluva lot of fun."

SK PEOPLE AROUND GREEN BAY FOR THEIR FAVORITE FAVRE memory, and you'll get countless anecdotes but rarely any hesitation. So many elite athletes captivate with their otherworldly physical gifts, but the common theme among the Favre highlights is the human element.

Jennifer Walentowski, Anna's mother: "In the Super Bowl against the Patriots, Brett threw a beautiful touchdown in the very beginning of the game, and he was so excited, he started running around the field. He had taken off his helmet, and he had both arms in the air, and there was such genuine joy on his face, such realness. Gosh, I'm tearing up right now just thinking about it."

Doug Phillips, whose daughter, Carley, participates in the Miracle League: "He hurt his ankle pretty bad against the Vikings [in 1995]. No one knew if he would play the next game [against Chicago]. He was on crutches all week, doubtful right up to kick-off. When he ran out of the tunnel at Lambeau, that was the loudest explosion I have ever heard in my life. And of course Brett threw five touchdowns that day."

Pete D'Amico, cofounder of the Door County Gulf Coast Relief Fund: "I lost my father a month before Brett's dad died. That Monday-night game against Oakland, the day after Big Irv died? I was crying that whole game. Just bawling. I know a lot of other people were too for their own reasons."

Donald Driver: "My favorite moment is from that Monday night against the Raiders, but it didn't happen on the field. Before the game I went to talk to Brett in his hotel room. He was hurting, obviously, but said he was going to play because we were his family too. It was pure love, pure brotherhood."

Sue LeTourneau of the Brian LaViolette Scholarship Foundation: "On his 30th birthday, I held up a sign in the stands here at Lambeau. When he ran onto the field, he looked at me and gave a thumbs-up. Oh, my God, I thought I was going to die right then and there!"

Mark Tauscher, Packers tackle: "My rookie year [2000] we were at Minnesota late in the year. Big game. At some point in the second half we were facing third down, and [center] Frank Winters misses a linebacker coming on a blitz. Brett gets sacked, but instead of jogging off the field he turns and chucks the ball at Frankie. And Frankie says, 'Well, get rid of the damn ball faster next time!' The whole team was laughing. It kind of loosened us up, and we went on to win."

Mike McCarthy: "In '99, when I was quarterbacks coach, three of the first four games were comebacks in the final couple of minutes. The one that stands out was against Tampa Bay. There's about a minute left, and we call this play where if the rush comes, Brett's supposed to check down to the back. Of course Tampa comes with everything they've got, but Brett just stands in there and throws a strike to Antonio Freeman for the winning touchdown, just as John Lynch and half the defense hits him in the jaw. On the sideline Brett's a little woozy; he's on oxygen; and I go up to him and say, 'What happened to the check down?' He says, 'Dammit, I forgot all about that. But, hey, I made the throw.' That's Brett Favre in a nutshell—he'll take the beating, but he'll always make the throw."

Ask Favre for his own favorite memory, and he is quiet for a moment. "I've got so many plays running through my mind," he says, finally. "The funny thing is, it's not only about the touchdowns and the big victories. If I were to make a list, I would include the interceptions, the sacks, the really painful losses. Those times when I've been down, when I've been kicked around, I hold on to those. In a way those are the best times I've ever had, because that's when I've found out who I am. And what I want to be." ✦

WALTER IOOSS JR.

 HERE TODAY Life after football was the last thing on Favre's mind in the fall of '07.

# WINTER WONDERLAND

BY PETER KING

*The snow fell at Lambeau on a perfect day for playoff football—and for Favre and his legion of fans, it was a blizzard of joy*

SI, JANUARY 21, 2008

**OULD YOU SAY THE BLESSING,** Breleigh?" Deanna Favre said on the Thursday night before the Packers' NFC divisional playoff game, and her eight-year-old daughter earnestly cast her eyes toward the floor in thought. A day shy of her half-birthday, Breleigh, a bubbly, ponytailed blonde, had much to be thankful for. "God," she said, matter-of-factly, "thank you for this food tonight, and thank you for my family and friends, and please help us beat Seattle, and please let us win the Super Bowl, and please let me have a happy half-birthday tomorrow." ✦ Hard to believe, but Brett Favre feels more pressure from his young daughter than he does from a premier NFL pass rush. Sacks he can take—439 of them in his 17-year career—but he hates seeing Breleigh upset after a loss, something he admits to thinking about on the rare occasions when games were going south this season. ✦ "She can't make it easy on me, can she?" Favre said after one of the

SIMON BRUTY

SNOWBALL'S CHANCE In what were clearly Favreable playoff conditions, Number 4 was magic.

SIMON BRUTY

The Frozen Tundra lived up to its billing in the Seahawks game, but the Packers were cool with it.

most memorable games of his Hall of Fame career, a 42–20 playoff victory over the Seattle Seahawks in the snow globe that was Lambeau Field. "I honestly don't want to disappoint her. You know how kids can be. I don't want her to go to school and have other kids say to her, 'Your dad stinks.' Which has happened."

Not lately. Favre, 38, has led the youngest team in the NFL to a 14–3 record and within one win of reaching Super Bowl XLII. "Did I ever think we'd be in this position?" Favre said, after the locker room had cleared out. "Quite honestly, no. I looked at us in the summer, and we were young at receiver, young at tight end, young in spots on the line. In the past, I knew every game what would work and how we'd win. Now I really have no idea week to week what's going to go well and what isn't. I'm thrilled about it, but it is a strange year. I'm just riding the wave."

On game day, the snow that began falling early created a near whiteout in the second half. But Favre was impervious to the conditions. He completed 18 of 23 passes on the day (two were dropped) for 173 yards, with three touchdowns and no interceptions. The offensive line overcame treacherous footing and held the cat-quick Seahawks' front seven to one sack and three quarterback pressures. Best of all, running back Ryan Grant, who was traded by the New York Giants to Green Bay on Sept. 1 for a sixth-round pick, recovered from losing two fumbles on his first three touches to run for a team playoff record 201 yards and score three touchdowns.

Grant's ascension—five 100-yard rushing games in the regular season after taking over the number 1 job in Week 8—transformed the Packers from the worst rushing team in the league after seven weeks to one that fits the philosophy of coach Mike McCarthy, who calls the plays. "I'd run it 50 times a game if I could; that would be a perfect game," McCarthy said before the game. Against Seattle, Green Bay ran on 35 of 59 offensive snaps (59%) and averaged a lusty 6.7 yards per carry.

Though Grant's lost possessions quickly put the Packers in a 14–0 hole, McCarthy said he didn't consider pulling his 6' 1", 224-pound back, who had fumbled only once in 218 regular season touches, because he was such an integral part of the game plan. "Who gives a [bleep]?" Favre told a downcast Grant on the sideline. "We're going to keep handing it to you." On the next six drives the 25-year-old Grant—a slashing, physical north-south runner—punished the Seahawks with 155 rushing yards; Green Bay scored on each of those possessions, running up its final 22-point margin with 13 minutes left in the game.

FIVE MONTHS AGO GRANT, A PART-TIME STARTER AS A SENIOR at Notre Dame in 2004 who went undrafted the following spring, was fifth on the Giants' depth chart. Now he's the hottest back in the playoffs. "When I watch him I see a hungry runner," said All-Pro LaDainian Tomlinson, who caught some of Grant's performance after his San Diego Chargers arrived in Indianapolis for their AFC playoff game. "The key to being a great back is that hunger."

You can say the same about passers. The night before the game Seattle coach Mike Holmgren, who had mentored Favre in Green Bay for seven seasons, said his defense "has to hit Brett a lot. I love him like a son, but we've got to hit him and disrupt his rhythm." The Seahawks, who were fourth in the NFL in sacks in 2007, with 45, couldn't do it. Even when they were able to flush him from the pocket, Favre would pull out another highlight-tape play like this one late in the first half:

From the shotgun on third-and-eight at the Seattle 14, Favre brought tight end Donald Lee into the backfield as the play clock ran down to :01. At the snap, defensive tackle Brandon Mebane shot through a gap and got his hands on the quarterback. But Favre wheeled away, stumbling to his right, and as he fell he underhanded the ball to Lee for an 11-yard gain. Instead of having to settle for a field goal attempt, Green Bay got a three-yard touchdown run from Grant on the next play to give the Pack a 28–17 lead at halftime.

"It's funny," Favre said afterward. "You would have thought I had played in a bunch of these games, but this was my first one where it snowed the whole game. I always wanted to play when it snowed so much you couldn't see the field. How great was that? I had the time of my life out there." ✦

# Green Bay Packers: *The* FAVRE

• 2007 | Favre led the Pack out against the Chargers.

JOHN BIEVER

MILWAUKEE • WISCONSIN
JOURNAL SENTINEL
jsonline.com
Miller
GENUINE Draft
COLD-FILTERED
JOHN DEERE
PACKERS
TO
RUSH
TOTAL
PASS
3:15:51 PM
Down
Yds to Go
Ball On
4 Quarter
0:02
RETIRED NUMBERS
14
DON HUTSON
3
TONY CANADEO
END ZONE

JOHN BIEVER

• 2007 | A 16–13 win over the Eagles at Lambeau in Week 1 kicked the season off right.

MIKE ROEMER/AP

• 1998 | A few die-hards took in Super Bowl XXXII from the comfort of the Lambeau lot.

JOHN BIEVER (2)

• 1993 | Packers newcomer Reggie White *(above)* and Favre, in his second Green Bay season, took the traditional training camp ride on young fans' bikes.

4

• 2004 | The Pack huddled around its leader during a January playoff game in Philadelphia, Favre's 19th postseason appearance.

DAVID BERGMAN

73

SIMON BRUTY (LEFT); ALLEN FREDRICKSON/REUTERS

• 2008 *left* | Brett gets set to launch during the NFC title game. • 2007 *above* | Ryan Grant's emergence gave Number 4 a new favorite in the backfield.

• 1997 | On the way to Super Bowl XXXI, Dorsey Levens and the Pack slogged past the Niners in a January divisional playoff.

JOHN BIEVER

• 1996 *above* | Favre completed 21 of 28 in a January playoff win at San Francisco.
• 1995 *right* | The Packers quarterback picked apart the Lions in October.

JOHN W. MCDONOUGH (LEFT); TOM G. LYNN

JEFF HANISCH/US PRESSWIRE

• 2005 | Favre was forced to flash his tackling skills in a Week 3 game against Tampa Bay.

TODD ROSENBERG/US PRESSWIRE (LEFT); STEVE JACOBSON

• 2005 *above* | Rod Gardner skied against Chicago on Christmas. • 2005 *right* | Kevin Barry and Vonta Leach shared the love after a TD pass against the Bucs.

Riddell
4
LEACH
48
PACKERS

92

©HUCK RYDLEWSKI/WIREIMAGE.COM (LEFT); JOHN BIEVER

• 1994 *left* | Reggie White made his move during a win over the Rams. • 1997 *above* | The future Hall of Famer blocked the Panthers' path in the playoffs.

JAMES V. BIEVER/WIREIMAGE.COM (LEFT); PETER READ MILLER

• 1994 *above* | Brett scored the game-winner in the Pack's County Stadium swan song. • 2002 *right* | The Niner's Chike Okeafor got a handful of Favre.

Riddell
4
OKEAFOR

SCOTT AUDETTE/AP (LEFT); AL GOLDIS/AP

• 2002 *above* | Tampa Bay's Simeon Rice took down Favre in a Bucs win. • 2003 *right* | Brett's 185th straight start was a typically tough showdown with Detroit.

• 2001 | Against the Ravens at Lambeau, a handoff to Ahman Green (30) got rough up front.

HEINZ KLUETMEIER

TOM HAUCK/GETTY IMAGES (LEFT); TODD ROSENBERG/GETTY IMAGES

• 2000 *above* | Favre signaled for timeout—or was it help?—in a loss to the Jets. • 1994 *right* | Sterling Sharpe was all smiles in a victory over the Vikes.

SCOTT
38
58
84

PACKERS
TO 3 RUSH
TOTAL 0 PASS
PM
Go
PACKERS

• 2005 | Before a January playoff game, Favre and fans marked the death of Reggie White.

4

TOM DIPACE (LEFT); AL TIELEMANS (TOP); DAMIAN STROHMEYER

• 1997 | In Super Bowl XXXI at the Superdome in New Orleans, Favre *(opposite)* joyfully celebrated his first touchdown pass, a 54-yarder to Andre Rison *(left)*; afterwards Rison and friends helped coach Mike Holmgren to a well-deserved victory ride.

JOHN BIEVER

• 2007 | Under heavy pressure in Minnesota, Number 4 unloaded in the direction of Donald Driver (80).

65
Riddell
WAYNE
55
adidas

JOHN BIEVER (LEFT); PATRICK FERRON/GREEN BAY PRESS-GAZETTE/AP

• 2002 *left* | Nate Wayne and the D put the wraps on the Niners in the playoffs. • 1998 *above* | Tennessee's Frank Wycheck got a love tap from Reggie White.

MORRY GASH/AP (LEFT); JOHN IACONO

• 1996 *above* | Dorsey Levens rumbled through the Vikings in December. • 1992 *right* | A young Favre led the Pack past the Steelers in his first NFL start .

• 2002 | Favre and defensive end James Hall gazed downfield after the QB had narrowly avoided a sack in a November win over the Lions.

JOHN BIEVER

Riddell

•1998 | In his seventh Packers season, a fleet Favre scrambled free against Tennessee.

JOHN BIEVER

87

SIMON BRUTY (3)

• 2008 | A mid-January blizzard in Green Bay provided the perfect setting for a playoff victory over the Seahawks, with cornerback Al Harris *(opposite)*, wideout Ruvell Martin *(above)* and defensive end Cullen Jenkins *(left)* among the Packers who enjoyed a snow day at Lambeau.

JONATHAN FERREY/GETTY IMAGES

• 2006 | Favre barked out the call in a November game against the Seahawks in Seattle.

JAMES V. BIEVER

• 2006 | He didn't invent the Lambeau Leap, but Favre took the plunge after a touchdown pass against the Cardinals in October.

TOM DAHLIN/WIREIMAGE.COM (LEFT); JOHN BIEVER

• 2006 *left* | Favre gave his all in a late-season win over the Vikings. • 2003 *below* | Brett and the boys were stunned by Atlanta at Lambeau in January—the first home playoff loss in Packers history.

FROM LEFT: JIM MONE/AP; HEINZ KLUETMEIER; JAMES V. BIEVER

• 1995 *left* | A week after spraining his ankle in Minnesota, Favre would toss five TDs against the Bears. • 1999 *above* | A flak jacket offered some protection from the pass rush. • 1992 *right* | The legend was born in a stirring last-minute win against Cincy; few remember the five sacks Favre suffered that day.

BRIAN BAHR/GETTY IMAGES

• 2003 | Anyway you slice it, Cheesehead Nation is vast—as the Cardinals discovered when they hosted Favre and the Pack for an early-season game in Arizona.

• 1996 *left and above* | Favre played it cool as the Pack readied for the playoffs. • 1995 | The opening of camp in July was cause for some showboating *(top)* and for sharing a smile with Reggie White *(right)*.

CLOCKWISE FROM LEFT: GARY PORTER/MILWAUKEE JOURNAL SENTINEL/AP; ROBERTO BOREA/AP (2); MORRY GASH/AP

4
91

• 2006 | Favre stood his ground in the middle during an October game against the Rams.

VERNON BIEVER/WIREIMAGE.COM

KIRBY LEE/US PRESSWIRE (LEFT); GREEN BAY PRESS-GAZETTE/AP (BELOW); WALTER IOOSS JR.

• 2007 *above* | A house backing onto Lambeau made tailgating a snap. • 2000 *right* | As always, the Pack attracted sellout crowds that included all forms of Wisconsin wildlife. • 1998 *far right* | Favre played the ham during a commercial shoot at a Texas supermarket.

Wilson
Sprite

• 2003 | Tony Fisher got the usual hands-on welcome in the stands after catching a Favre touchdown pass in September.

JONATHAN DANIEL/GETTY IMAGES

JOHN BIEVER (LEFT); HEINZ KLUETMEIER

• 1999 | Lions cornerback Robert Bailey *(above)* and Vikings linebacker Dwayne Rudd *(right)* were two of the many defenders anxious to get a piece of Number 4, who was sacked 35 times in '99.

Riddell
4

JOHN BIEVER

• 2008 | The Packers' O-line set up a wall for Ryan Grant during the January division-round playoff game against the Seahawks.

• 2002 *above* | For once Favre was on the receiving end of a record, when the Giants' Michael Strahan set the single-season sack mark in a January game with the Packers. • 2004 *right* | The agony was evident after an interception against the Jaguars in December. • 2007 *far right* | Even in a 34–0 rout of the Vikings, Favre occasionally found himself on dangerous ground.

PETER CARR/THE JOURNAL NEWS (TOP); DAVID STLUKA/GETTY IMAGES (LEFT); JOHN BIEVER

RICH FRISHMAN (LEFT); WALTER IOOSS JR.

• 1995 *left* | Favre found respite from football in his favorite off-field pursuit. • 1994 *above* | The hunter posed during a photo shoot at the Pro Bowl.

JOHN BIEVER

• 2002 | William Henderson (33) led the way for Najeh Davenport against the Lions.

JOHN BIEVER (MARINO); MICHAEL HICKEY/WIREIMAGE.COM (MANNING); JOHN IACONO (ELWAY); HEINZ KLUETMEIER (BRADY); PETER READ MILLER (YOUNG)

• 1997 *top* | Favre and Dan Marino at Lambeau. • 2004 *left* | Peyton Manning had the edge in Indy. 1998 *center* | With John Elway before Super Bowl XXXII. • 2005 *right* | A laugh with Tom Brady. • 1998 *opposite* | Favre and Steve Young after the NFC title game.

Riddell
YOUN
8
4

ERIC GAY/AP (LEFT); STEVE JACOBSON

• 1995 *above* | Mark Ingram offered a helping hand against Dallas. • 2004 *right* | The visiting Jaguars got a good look at Favre's sometimes gravity-defying style.

4

• 1997 | A little snow didn't keep 60,000 Lambeau faithful from celebrating the return of the Packers—and the Lombardi Trophy—after Super Bowl XXXI.

TIM ZIELENBACH/AFP

• 2006 | The familiar smile peeked out before the Pack took on Seattle on New Year's Day.

TODD ROSENBERG/US PRESSWIRE

Riddell

• 2007 | At age 38 Favre remained the beating heart of the Packers and an object of admiration extending far beyond the stands in Green Bay.

ERIC ESPADA/CAL SPORT MEDIA

JOHN BIEVER

• 1996 | A packed house at Lambeau Field saw Favre help beat the archrival Bears 28–17.

BRETT FAVRE HAS BEEN ONE OF SPORTS ILLUSTRATED'S MOST exhaustively covered athletes. Dozens of the magazine's writers, photographers and editors have documented his career, and the stories and pictures collected here represent their cumulative effort. Our thanks go out to them. Special thanks, as well, to Stefanie Kaufman, who provided tireless organizational help; David Bauer for his deft guidance; Walter Iooss Jr., Vernon Biever, John Biever and James Biever for opening up their photo archives; the SI imaging department for its exceptional work; and SI Group editor Terry McDonell for providing the inspiration and the resources to get the project done.

Lastly, this list would not be complete if we did not express our gratitude to the real stars of this project: Brett and Deanna Favre, who, in times both triumphant and trying, have so graciously allowed SI into their lives.

JOHN BIEVER; FRONT FLAP MAGAZINE COVERS, CLOCKWISE FROM TOP LEFT: SIMON BRUTY; WALTER IOOSS JR.; PETER READ MILLER; WALTER IOOSS JR.; BACK FLAP MAGAZINE COVERS, CLOCKWISE FROM TOP LEFT: WALTER IOOSS JR.; AL TIELEMANS; JOHN W. MCDONOUGH; RICHARD CORMAN